Henri Bourgeois

ON BECOMING CHRISTIAN

Christian initiation
and its sacraments

TWENTY-THIRD PUBLICATIONS
Mystic, Connecticut

Original title: *L'initiation chretienne et ses sacraments*
© 1982 Editions du Centurions, Paris

Translated by Dame Mary Groves, O.S.B., Oulton Abbey

English translation copyright © 1984
by St Paul Publications
Middlegreen, Slough SL3 6BT England
First published February 1984

North American edition 1985
by Twenty-Third Publications
P.O. Box 180
Mystic CT 06355
(203) 536-2611

ISBN 0-89622-270-5 (paper)
     0-89622-271-3 (cloth)

Library of Congress Catalog Card Number 85-51084

Cover design by William Baker

Contents

Do we always have to be interested in other people's baptisms? Our own children's and the baptisms of other people's children? Is there no need to think back on the baptism we have ourselves received?

Is it sensible to put in a great deal preparing and animating first communion celebrations while not making a comparable effort over baptism and confirmation?

Should we go on speaking of baptism, confirmation and first communion without sufficiently insisting on the links between these three sacraments and without asking ourselves how all three make a complementary contribution to initiation into the christian faith?

Has the time come to give confirmation a more definite connotation in spite of the obscurities at this juncture?

Are we to go on much longer regarding baptism as solely a sacrament for babies, forgetting that our churches also celebrate baptism for adults and school-children?

This book would like to give something of an answer to these and some other problems. And add a glimmer of hope.

Introduction

The publication of the *Rite for the Christian Initiation of Adults* and of the new *Rite for the Baptism of Infants* was an event of considerable importance. The pastoral realisation of these rites however has caused those responsible some problems. These include difficulties in understanding the thrust of these liturgies — for to some the theological terrain is unfamiliar. There are also sometimes awkward practical difficulties — old comfortable ceremonies are abandoned, ministers and participants are required to do and say things where meaning is not immediately plain. To some the new rites appear to be just another annoying change; or a piece of liturgical archaeology; or at best a clearer and more effective presentation of the old ceremonies. One of the virtues of Henri Bourgeois' book is that it scotches the notion that the changes involved in these rites are merely decorative — the kind of thing enthusiastic amateurs go in for. The sacraments of initiation provide a profound, though not discursive answer to the question: what is it to be a christian and how does a person become one.

I was brought up to believe that the answer to that question could be given in a few simple doctrinal formulas; about original sin, sanctifying grace, redemption and sacramental causality. The risk involved in pinning too much of our christian understanding to doctrinal formulas is that it may become superficially cognitive and distorted; pastorally, it can lead us badly astray. We may be led to work as though these were an order of supernatural events almost completely separate from human experience and growth. A theology which speaks in the language of human experience, however, contains its own danger. It is that of reducing sacraments to human processes, of obscuring the sovereign initiative of God. It is the danger of 'psychologising' the sacraments and once we begin to use the language of human growth it is difficult to get firm ground under our feet. The liturgy, being a quite different language of faith, avoids this dilemma. It speaks to us not in facts but in mysteries and in this idiom the acts of God and the experience of human persons do not occur in different registers. It is a question, our author says, of "becoming what we are" of growing humanly into the condition which God's saving love has already graciously established.

Being and becoming a christian has become much more problematic in recent years. The formerly powerful forces of family tradition, christian culture, social pressure, are much weakened. It is true that parents often bring their children to baptism for these reasons. They are not bad reasons, but we are left nowadays with an uneasy feeling that what baptism does will not humanly be upheld. Moreover many people nowadays, especially the young, seem to make their spiritual journey without much reference to ecclesiastical structure and pathways. "On the one hand the fact, on the other the Church". On the one hand the established progression of the initiating sacraments, on the other the untidy, sprawling, unpredictable process of the growth of human persons. These are the reasons why we need to grasp the inner logic of the initiating sacraments more profoundly.

Henri Bourgeois' book throws a lot of light on these problems. It contains no neat answers though it offers some useful suggestions. Most of all it provides a historical and theological perspective within which many problems appear in a different and clearer light. One of these is: how should we prepare for the baptism of babies, how ready should we be to baptise? Should we see baptism as readily and unquestioningly available or as something of great price which has to be worked for? What about confirmation, a sacrament, many say, in search of a theology? Is its theology best found in its history? How can first communion be presented more effectively as one of the sacraments of initiation? Finally, how can these sacraments be held together as a single initiating process? Ought we not to have generally within the Church, a more baptismal outlook, making memorial of our baptism, reactivating it in the other sacraments and in other ways. And what would be the implications of catechists, parents and priests if this initiating outlook were widespread and fundamental? Would it not re-kindle among us something of the newness, the unquenchable freshness of early days?

The connection is clear with the teaching of *Catechesi Tradendae* and of the *General Catechetical Directory*. The Church should be a catechetical community. Its catechetical task is more than its packaging department. It is a task through which the Church constantly renews itself. Time and again it celebrates the mystery of God's saving love and truth in the world. Time and again it draws in new members, leads them into the mysteries of the faith, liberates and incorporates their gifts, makes them part of the body of Christ through which God's universal and creative word is uniquely and luminously made flesh.

Kevin Nichols
26.8.1983

1

To be christian
you have to become one

Christians are not born but made

Often, it must be admitted, people are *chance* christians: they have come into the world in a good christian family where the religion is handed on, along with the family name and language.

But does chance arrange everything for the best? Is that enough to make a christian?

Admittedly, in the ordinary state of affairs I am describing here, people are not christians by pure chance. A person is a christian, too, through *love*, and even in some cases through *faith*. Parents presenting their children for baptism do it in order to hand on their own religious affiliation. Vague, often enough. And yet it is to be found in some families bound up with truly christian conviction and experience.

But even in such cases, which are not all that frequent, the love and faith of the parents are stamped on the new baby as a characteristic feature. Then the question will surely arise: Are you a christian because you have been made one?

Often, too, we are christian from habit: we might not have been, we could stop being, but we carry on by the force of momentum.

But is habit to be confused with faith?

As a christian of the third century, Tertullian, said, in a well-known phrase: "One is not *born* but *becomes* a christian"[1]. He wanted to underline here that no one is automatically a christian. For him, the fact of being a christian was not necessarily implied in being human, even if the condition of being human did have something "naturally christian" about it. Christianity was gift, event. And it was the action of baptism which exhibited that gratuitousness, that contingency.

On reading today this remark from a christian of former times, we might want to alter it a little. For since then things have changed rather, at least in countries where christianity is of long standing.

Of course, baptism continues in theory an event distinguishing the birth of a human being and not to be confused with it: 'We are not born christian'. But in practice it is very often included along with the family rituals marking a child's coming into the world. It is a fact,

1. De testimonio animae, I — fieri non nasci solet christiana.

more than a becoming. So much so that Tertullian's phrase could be put thus: 'We are made a christian, we have to become one'.

In other words: people are christian by birth, by chance, by love, perhaps by faith, and have to become so by their history. That is to say by having the opportunity or the will to choose and to ratify what circumstances or family tradition have allowed.

I should like for the moment merely to emphasise briefly that the baptism which makes a christian, which makes a person be christian, could well have also a role in this becoming a christian which I am suggesting.

Becoming a christian

We should not be deceived however. To emphasise as I am doing the historical becoming called for by the christian faith does not amount to minimising the content of faith. To be christian certainly presupposes that we become one. But christian faith is never 100% clear understanding and free adherence. It is both social and individual. It occurs as a given fact.

Furthermore there is always a danger in these matters of exalting one culture and from that generalising as valid for all peoples the forms of conscientious decision and free-will pertaining to limited groups who value personal autonomy. Becoming christian does not happen in the same way for all christians.

But, providing we do not lose sight of these important distinctions, it is possible to say that the christian faith normally implies at some point taking a *personal stand*. We are not christian solely because of others: we are so by reason of an accepted present and a desired future.

I must repeat, this 'individuation' of the faith can have very different styles. It remains in some cases very social, very much bound up with environment or belonging to a group. In other cases it takes rather the form of a decision and a conversion which hardly depend on background. But however we look at it, we are not christian without sooner or later following a road from the given fact to the desired fact. We may have been a christian until then. Now we have to become one, at least to some extent, from now on.

This 'becoming' does not always happen, so far as can be judged. Numbers of our contemporaries do not appear to have had the opportunity or the taste for taking on the tradition of belief in which they were enrolled at birth. They call themselves christians, certainly. And so they are, since they have been made christians. Again, to the extent to which they are attached to the christianity of their family tradition and share in some christian beliefs and practices. But they do not become christian. Or at least they do so in limited fashion, not fully. And this raises an essential question: What is the point, then, of being a christian, and not becoming one in practice?

Several ways of becoming christian?

All the same there are nowadays certain relatively new factors which lead me to re-examine the accepted way of understanding 'becoming' a christian.

First of all the social 'edge' christianity had traditionally, and which made it normal and even rightful, has for many people no longer the same importance. Formerly people were christian almost '*a priori*'. Today, force of habit is diminishing. In consequence a person who was made a christian once, either ceases to practice or is driven to becoming one. In both cases the *slightest social pressure* alters the matter. I do not intend here to determine whether the change is good or bad. I shall content myself with noting it. It seems to me to have contrasting effects: some are turned away from all individuation of the faith, while others are drawn to it.

Further, a voluntary and therefore relatively knowledgeable approach to the christian faith is at the moment taking on aspects which would formerly have been played down or even challenged. Ordinarily, 'conscious' believers were the same as the practising. So they are still, quite often. But since the last war they are also seen as being among the militants, with this difference that not all militant christians are necessarily practising, at least in the traditional sense. Today it could even be that some are 'becoming' christians without being *in actual fact* practising or militant.

This certainly raises problems. But it requires us nevertheless to pay attention to quite significant phenomena in the present age: groups foreign to the Churches or clearly marginal in regard to them, being drawn to religious values through the media and therefore without entering a concrete community of believers, ways of self-taught christians, fashion for studying the christian phenomenon in depth in terms of oriental spiritualities, etc.

Finally, a third factor at the present time, approach to the christian faith is not effected only on the basis of an acquired factor such as family tradition or baptism given at birth. Today in the old christian countries adults come to the faith fully aware, without being brought to it by a past history entirely under the aegis of christianity. They are not 'born' christians. *They become so before being so*, when the usual way is to become so having been so. They desire baptism and communion, ask to be received into a Church. All this as adults. They are catechumens. And their witness requires from now on to be taken into account.

Approach to the christian faith

How do you become a christian?

This is the question that the present book seeks to answer.

The problem has, as will have been seen, several aspects.

First of all, what is the connection between fact and becoming in the christian experience? The modern tendency, hooked on subjective values, is to emphasise the becoming. To the extent of bracketting out the fact, as though almost ashamed of it: you are not made christian, it is a becoming. This shows itself notably in a certain doubt about the sacrament, suspected of promoting the fact to the detriment of the historical becoming. Or again, from a reluctance to declare themselves christians, some today say they are not sure, or claim to be searching, and will not accept to be stuck fast in the fact of a recognised and recognisable identity.

Next, approach to the christian faith, its becoming, is not necessarily today found in the framework of an ecclesial institution. Whether they were made christians at the beginning of their life or whether they were not baptised, some of our contemporaries are seeking their way without having recourse to the programmes and itineraries marked out by the Churches. Hence the question which cannot be ignored by the christian groups: What is the meaning of an 'initiation' into christianity? What are its genuinely indispensable elements? Why have to be a church member in order to be a follower of Jesus? Once again the sacramental factor finishes off the inquiry. For the sacrament brings in the Church. What are the grounds for its place in christian initiation?

Celebrations

On the one hand the fact, on the other the Church: it is in this field it seems to me, the future of the christian faith should be considered today.

And it is in this perspective that I should like to adopt here a standpoint which is restricted but fundamental. I shall consider approach to the faith under the aspect of the celebrations which in the common ecclesial tradition are thought necessary structures. In other words I shall take my stand in view of the sacraments.

It will be seen why. It appears to me that the sacraments pose the two lines of inquiry just referred to and bring them together. For they stamp us with the fact of christianity while claiming that this given fact leads on to and arouses confessional faith. And at the same time they stamp us with the fact of the Church while asserting that this ecclesial fact gives shape and opportunity to a most individual faith.

How can that be?

Initiation and the sacraments

Certainly we do not become christian through the sacraments alone. We become christian also through many other factors, all of which are part of the mystery of the faith in us. These factors are not unlimited in number. Whatever may be in actual fact the variety of roads to be followed, however irreducible the mystery of each existence, there are a few recognisable constants to be pinpointed as intervening in a person's journey towards individual faith. This is so true that we notice it when this or that factor is missing. As though the lack of it conflicts with what is customary.

These factors guiding the development of faith I should like to list briefly as: the occasion which starts off the process of becoming christian, the past which necessarily influences what is to follow either to facilitate or to hamper the movement begun, catechesis leading to spiritual discovery of the Gospel and the christian heritage, the group of believers with whom the person enters into effective relations, the celebrations at intervals along the route, the personal experience which catechesis and celebrations are intended to frame but which always remains unpredictable and unique in style.

In this complex, the sacraments — normally, according to the christian tradition — have their place. They are certain particular ceremonies: not all the celebrations which help to becoming a christian are sacramental. Their originality lies in linking up the fact and the becoming. They stamp us, our body even, with the experience of a developing faith which will continue to expand. They integrate into the Church, and in the name of the Church modify the life of a being discovering christianity. They are felt by believers as an action of God himself, thus attesting that God is always taking part in the process under way.

Of the christian sacraments baptism, confirmation and first communion play a fundamental role in christian being and becoming. They structure the faith and give it objectivity. So they are called sacraments of initiation.[1]

The formula is a happy one. For these three sacraments concentrate and make explicit what the Church offers to those who are becoming christians. Their role is to lay the foundation of christian personality. They lead into the order of mystery to which none can have entry by their own strength, the order of gospel faith and church life.

Initiation according to the sacraments

Who does not see the difficulties arising from such a programme?

1. A term in initiation with present-day connotations unknown to the early christians and the Middle Ages.

I have indicated them already.

The first is regarding the Church. The sacraments of initiation affirm that we cannot become christian without entering the Church and joining the Church. They do not adopt a position on what the Church concretely is in its various forms. But they maintain that the Church is first of all and before all the grouping in which we are made christian, and in which we become what we are.

The second difficulty bears on the sacramental phenomenon itself, on the possibility of translating faith into fact at a given time in a life, and on the chances this fact has of introducing an effective christian becoming. Are not the sacraments of christian initiation on the side of custom, more than on the side of free-will and conscious decision? They can be said to accompany christian becoming. But, in fact, they integrate it into a given state of things. Can they be expected to orientate towards becoming a christian after having been made a christian?

The sacraments of initiation today

Modern thinking on the three sacraments of initiation is proving abundant. As though the multiplicity of trials and experiments have brought into relief the difficulties which crop up.

A first line of thought is of the *pastoral type*. It is a question of helping christians, at their various levels of response, to understand what it is that they are celebrating. How can parents asking for their children to be baptised enter into the meaning of the sacrament? How can christians preparing parents for the baptism of their child or preparing infants and young people for the eucharist and for confirmation set about it trying to do as little harm as possible, taking into account the ambiguous nature of many of the requests for the sacraments? How celebrate christian initiation by means of sacramental signs in the context of a country like ours today, with its diversities, social, cultural and spiritual, as we know? The effort called for in this way is at once catechetical, liturgical, and in the end evangelising. Quite often it turns out to be theological at the same time. For example, many people today are seeking to comprehend better and in their deeper connection the various effects which the christian tradition attributes to the sacraments of initiation.

Another line of thought on these sacraments at the present time, less important from the point of view of the volume of debate and study but most suggestive and stimulating, is in the *ecumenical* order. The aim then is to bring about exchanges between the various susceptibilities found in christianity by considering their historical traditions.

Without at all minimising these two perspectives, complementary in any case, I should like to subscribe here to another viewpoint. It appears to me actually that pastoral thinking and ecumenical dialogue are held up, if the sacraments of initiation are 'other people's sacraments' only, for those who receive them and no longer present realities for the christians who have received them already. Therefore I should like to urge a *reactivation* of the sacraments of initiation in the spiritual experience of actual christians. In the conviction that these rites are never done with producing their effects, and that they have not yet said their last word.

Reactivating what has ceased to operate

How in fact do we grasp sufficiently the implications of infant baptism if we lose the sense of baptism in ourselves? And how find in ecclesial communities a more 'true' way of celebrating confirmation if this sacrament has in practice no place in christian life, except precisely when we speak of confirming the very young?

In other words, modern christians ordinarily think of sacramental initiation *for* others besides themselves — children, young people — or *with* others besides themselves — parents wanting the sacraments for their children or else christians of another tradition — more than for *themselves*.

This is not without its difficulties. Baptism, for example, is indeed a part of pastoral responsibility. But could it not also be, much more than it is, a mystery to which each one relates in his or her personal or church life? And could it not constitute a spring at which the christian communities could renew themselves in the realisation of their identity and in thanksgiving?

Note also, by comparison with the little real care we have of baptism, the present practice with regard to first communion. People are certainly not lacking in a eucharistic sense. But for want of a sufficient baptismal sense, is not this taste for the eucharist marked with deficiencies? People are often massing christians but lose sight sometimes of the beginning of christian life, its birth, and that it sees itself as baptismal by recalling that origin, which is free gift. Perhaps people have too little baptismal sense, or too little experience of baptism to balance the eucharistic sense characteristic of contemporary christianity, notably in France.

Basically, their baptism once received is behind them. It is part of their past. It no longer has a place in their present. In the 20th century we are christians under the sign of a faith which is always fluctuating and needing continual renewal, under the sign of a fight for justice and liberty in the name of community, sharing, and the eucharist, but with very little reference to baptism. One simple indication: if someone asked you to say what a christian is, would it come to your mind to

B

answer: a baptised person? We do not think of that. Doubtless because we want to speak of mystery rather than about ritual. But also because we do not integrate our baptism in full consciousness.

Confirmation and the eucharist initiate
What I have just pointed out regarding baptism holds good, more or less, for confirmation and the eucharist.

Confirmation, even though experiencing lately a certain upswing, remains scarcely characteristic in christian life. Classic theology said that it marked christians with a character. But our contemporary experience gives little enough support to this statement of principle.

As for the eucharist, the place it holds in the personal and collective life of 'conscious' christians is obviously very great. But it is not so sure that the value for initiation is really obvious. Certainly we prepare children for communion: their first communion in the accepted phrase. That is to say the time when their faith, from then on initiated enough, is in a position to complete the basic course of its formation by communicating in the paschal mystery of Christ. But is that enough for the ecclesial community taken as a whole to consider the eucharist as initiating?

We may doubt it. If this were indeed the case it would occasionally be celebrated, and we should speak of it from time to time differently from the way that we do. Instead of understanding it in a somewhat one-sided fashion as an exercise or setting to work of a faith held to be already formed we should live it too, and perhaps first of all, as a growth point in gospel faith. To make one's communion would be to learn to believe; to receive from God that capacity for thanksgiving which is our faith. It would be to realise that we have mysteriously found in the water of baptism the cross of the Risen Lord and that there is all too little eucharistic bread and wine for absorbing this paschal mystery to which we are called to witness.

In the same way, instead of endlessly discussing ways of assimilating the eucharist to life as though the aforesaid eucharist was always and everywhere a nourishment, always in a position to take effect, we would begin by realising what it has of mysterious and even strange. A good way of grasping its original power would be to set it in the perspective of baptism. It would then be the finale to a hope begun in the waters of baptism. It would be an integral part of faith and not the occasion for an exercise of that faith.

I was saying just now that people have too little sense of baptism by comparison with the eucharistic sense that is theirs. Now I will add that their eucharistic sense is too much a sense of 'christianity' and not enough a sense of initiation.

Do you recall what you have received?

My intention therefore in this book is to seek to reactivate baptism and, in the same line of initiation, the eucharist and confirmation. For if we do not call to mind the sacraments which have made us christian, there is a great danger of not really knowing how to put these same sacraments to work with and for others.

You who prepare parents for their children's baptism, who take part in a baptism in your family, who are witnesses at an adult baptism, who baptise, are ministers of baptism, how is it with you and your baptism? What notice do you take of your own baptism?

You who prepare adolescents or young people for confirmation, who take part in a confirmation ceremony, how is it with you and your confirmation? Has confirmation marked you?

You who live by the eucharist, does it seem to you that this sacrament has formed your faith? And you who for all sorts of reasons say you find difficulty in taking part in the eucharistic celebration, do you think it can go on initiating you in your faith?

Therefore it is to an 'anamnesis'[1] that I am inviting you. Do you want by memory and by faith to reactivate those actions which gave you to be what you are?

This standpoint explains the style and tenor of this book. I have not wanted to write a treatise on the sacraments of initiation. There is no lack of excellent examples. I have not tried either to go into the details of the current pastoral or ecumenical debate, particularly in what concerns infant baptism. These questions are important certainly but they cannot occupy the whole field of priorities. Enough to stand back a little from all that. I have attempted to go back to a sacramental past which I am surprised is not more present. With the conviction that the contemporary Church needs such a memory as this. And with the hope that this reactivation may be of help to each one who will read these pages.

This book therefore is addressed to those with a christian past. As, in the framework of the Lyons catechumenate, I have accompanied adults on their way towards sacramental initiation, I indeed know that baptism, eucharist and confirmation are also a present reality and even a future hope for some people of our day. But now it has became clear to me that the experience of newcomers to the faith will not arrive at regenerating in the Church a true sense of initiation if those already christians, initiated from birth and childhood, do not rediscover the taste for recalling what made them christians.

* * *

1. This word, coming from the Greek, indicates the action of believers recalling a decisive event in their religious history and making it present.

Summary

I should like to collect up the main points of this first chapter as follows:

— I am speaking here of christian initiation by using the classic expression which conveniently characterises the *process* by which the faith is formed in a person opening to the Gospel.

— This initiation has two poles: one pole an established or acquired *fact* and one pole a *becoming* or free and conscious commitment to the following of Jesus. There is initiation precisely when these two poles link up and give value to their complementary significations. In other words, a person is not initiated into christianity except to the extent of experiencing that the faith is given to us and enters into us, while still remaining a forward movement and an adventure.

— Christian initiation likewise presents two other correlated aspects: it is *social* and *individual*. After a long period when the social and ecclesial aspect stood out as of major importance, we are probably entering on a time when the personal aspect is going to become strongly emphasized. In this context, to be initiated means realising how to accept oneself and a personal faith through a church allegiance which must, certainly, be defined, but which is not considered *a priori* as outside of the individual approach.

— Does christian initiation concern only those who are being initiated? Has it not also an importance for those who have been through the basic process but continue living it? My suggestion is that the *reactivation* of initiation can help to heal some of today's ills.

— In any case, christian initiation does *not consist solely* of the sacraments. If I am considering it here by reference to the three sacraments it is because they have a favourably strategic position. But it should be understood that the sacraments are not to be dissociated from the other elements without which the faith would never be initiated.

2

You have a better memory
than you think

Remembering or recalling?

For most of you I imagine, baptism is an event impossible to recall. You were baptised a few days or weeks after you were born. Impossible at that age to keep track consciously of what was happening to you then.

Besides it can be, as with some modern christians, that you find fault with the procedure of infant baptism. Or you know people who are in that position and regret having been baptised so early. I have often for my part heard this type of opinion expressed by 'old christians' to adults just baptised. You can see the point. Their regret is basically not to have been present at their baptism. They would like to have been conscious of it and therefore able to revive the memory of it. They do not want their children to miss it too.

I would rather not for the moment go into the question of infant baptism. We shall come to it, rest assured. But I merely make a note of this fact: no more than you can picture the time of your birth can you recall your baptism, in the ordinary sense of the word recall. You have been told about it, you have seen the written entry, you know that you were baptised, but it escapes you. This moment in your past will not respond to your call.

Is that necessarily upsetting? In any case, so it is. Of course those christians who have been baptised as adults, or, again, when of school-age, or else during their adolescent years, can consciously go back to the time of that celebration. But most christians cannot do this. And you are probably in that situation. You *know* you were baptised, you do not *remember* it.

However, for christianity, to have received baptism is not simply an item of knowledge. It belongs to *memory*. A somewhat paradoxical memory because it does not necessarily involve remembering.

Let me try to explain myself.

Believing is remembering

To understand what is implied, we have to make a 'detour' via the Bible. Biblical memory, like all religious memory, presents in effect two complementary forms whose inter-relation can throw light on the relationship we have with our baptism.

The first of these forms is fairly standard: people recall the past because of having been *witnesses* of events. This act of memory clearly takes on particular features. The faithful are recalling together certain major events which have marked them out as a people. And they do it especially in the course of celebrations or symbolic gestures giving form to their common memory. So it is for example when at Easter the scripture reading (Ex 12,14) presents as a point of reference for memory the liberation from Egypt.

But as time passed, witnesses of those decisive events disappeared. And yet the people itself went on. It *kept* in its faith *the imprint* of what had happened for it, continued living it. Here there is a second form of memory. Believers going back to a time in the past of which they can have no recall, properly speaking, but on which they rely and which they attest. They are remembering what they cannot recall.

It is this second form of memory which appears enlightening to me when we today want to refer back to our baptism. The event as such escapes us, we have no *recollection* of it. Given that the event in question remains in relation to us because it continues to mark us, and is linked with us through an historical continuity, that of the life of faith.

Scripture calls '*memorial*' a celebration of the past which cannot be recollected but whose presence is carefully preserved.

Easter Day is thus the memorial of the liberation from Egypt: "That day shall be for you a memorial day, and you shall keep it as a feast to the Lord; throughout your generations you shall observe it as an ordinance for ever" (Ex 12,14).

At the other end of the Bible, Paul continues this sense of memorial. Writing to new christians coming from hellenism he affirms that they have entered into the biblical tradition and have henceforth as their fathers those Hebrews who went through the sea under the leadership of Moses. On two occasions he emphasises the contemporary actuality of these founding events (1 Cor 10,6 and 11). The same structure develops between what Jesus lived and the life his disciples lived. Paul quotes the word from Maundy Thursday which explicitly charges christians to make a memorial of what Jesus said and did then: "Do this in remembrance of me" (1 Cor 11,24).

In the Bible consequently believing, that multi-dimensional act, is notably expressed through memory. The fidelity of the believers is rooted in that of God manifested from age to age. Hope and the expectation of the original and unheard-of acts of God are buttressed by a past whose power we can experience today.

What is faith-memory?

Before seeing what conditions may be required for a faith-memory of baptism it seems useful to underline why the Bible insists so much on memory and why it makes it one of the forms of faith.

If believers are invited to make a memorial, it is fundamentally because faith is not simply knowledge. To believe is to ratify the presence of yesterday in today. Believers are people in time. For them, today and tomorrow take their explanation from yesterday. In this sense, therefore, it is not enough to know oneself to be baptised nor even to know that one has been baptised. We must feel still today the driving-force of baptism once received. Consequently the experience entering in here has a double movement. It goes back to yesterday, refers back to what it was. But equally it brings the past to us, makes it actual, gives it a place and acceptance in our present. To know about one's baptism would therefore not be enough. We still have to make a remembrance of it.

Then again if it is possible to have a memory with no recollection, this is because recollection is not the determining factor in this case. What is decisive is the power of the past continuing to reach us. In other words it is God's commitment to his own, extending even to us, on the basis of what it was once for all in the past. Faith-memory has its foundation in the very action of God. It is not man recalling by force of memory, it is God giving to man the possibility of making remembrance in virtue of the Covenant which he makes with us.

Making a remembrance of God

Faith-memory witnesses therefore to the historicity of God present in that of the believers.

In other words, when we make remembrance we are believing in a God who willed to *be bound in time.* One day he willed to imprint on history a decisive, recognisable, mark of his presence. Since then he maintains this investment day by day. His continued nearness to humanity is on a line with what happened with Moses. Certainly, the christian faith professes that he has outstandingly added to his presence in his Son Jesus. But the incarnation of Christ does not cancel the mosaic event: it completes it. And biblically its significant reference is the liberating act of the Exodus.

All this orients our faith. We believe that God does not repeat himself. But equally we believe that he always acts in the same sense, with the creation and re-creation of mankind. So much so that we have to keep in our hearts what he has brought about from age to age. For this tradition about God indicates that the great divine acts, those founding and renewing the Covenant, are too full of meaning and universal significance to display all their effects at once.

Next, notice that the past gradually becoming actual in the faith present has a two-fold dimension. It is at the same time *mystery and event.* The mystery is God's commitment of what he has of fullest and most permanent. It is the divine action by which is communicated the very being of God. This mystery therefore widely affects history. It is, according to the received term, of the eschatological order. But it takes shape in history through events. Thus the Exodus. Here the liberation event witnesses to the liberating will of God. To celebrate Easter is therefore at once to evoke what is past and to invoke the presence of God at work yesterday and today. A remembrance consists in making real God's commitment through a founding event in which it is inscribed. By looking back to yesterday, believers are not straining over a past fact cut off from its significance of mystery, but going back to the divine mystery which was, and is, and is to come.

The duty of memorial

Finally I should like to remark that the believing memory is *not optional*. In the Bible it is a command of God. To make a remembrance is not a task left to our discretion and fancy. It is a duty, as it is an action vital for faith. A faith which forgets is no covenant faith. "That day, says God, shall be a memorial day".

In practice this obligation is fulfilled by means of the 'memorial', that is to say a symbolic moment, a significant gesture by which, through what God was yesterday, the believers contact what he still is today. Memorial has therefore the value of a sign. It is a regular and objective encounter with time. A special time for reliving and living. "Do this in memory of me".

Thus God asks his people to make remembrance by making a memorial. He wishes history to be strung at intervals with powerful commemorative moments so that life in its continuity should be one whole act of faith. This is how the believing memory is organised. It needs special times to enable it to be at work all the time. There are the feasts, there is that weekly feast which in judaism is the Saturday and in christianity the Sunday. But all this aims at arousing a continuous remembrance. We might therefore think of the memorial as a sacramental expression of faith-memory. At the moment and in the symbolic actions of the memorial are manifested God's faithful tradition and the believing memory of mankind.

God says: you will make memorial. He means: you will be creatures with a memory, beings whose faith takes the form of remembrance.

If you accept this analysis you will doubtless see how the sacramentality of the memorial operates. It presumes the faculty of memory. And at the same time it starts up this faculty in the believers. In this sense the memorial does not stop at making a remembrance. It also gives memory.

Letting baptism act

Making remembrance of the baptism we have received: What does that have to say to us?

Essentially it is a matter of conviction. For if we hardly ever remember our baptism it is probably because our faith has generally little taste for this sort of work. We imagine we can live without the past and without having to come to terms with it. We have a certain amount of knowledge of what has gone before us but it is more difficult for us to admit that we are the children of yesterday.

We have consequently to rediscover a side of our faith we do not know too well. It is a way of believing, to realise that we have begun to believe. It is a kind of pledge of our faith to remember our beginnings in the faith.

Making present the baptism we received once upon a time is not therefore simply trying to live as baptised persons. It is more than that. It is a question of allowing baptism, or rather the God of baptism, to act in our lives. By avoiding the sacrament being overlaid by other sacramental actions considered superior to it. Equally by trying for the baptismal act not to be blurred by the greyness and dullness of the everyday.

Put another way, we have to give baptism every 'chance'. We are called to live in a baptismal present. We are christians only by reactivating the way in which we were made christians. We cannot confirm our present steps in the faith except by not losing sight of our first steps in the faith.

The part played by the beginning

Why this continual return to the beginning? Is it out of a questionable nostalgia? It seems to me that it is rather by reason of the biblical experience.

And indeed, in the Bible the beginnings of faith are never forgotten. They are made present as a fundamental and in some sort a lasting moment. Moses, Abraham, are the contemporaries of every Jew. And Israel aimed even at portraying the beginning of the world in the imposing panorama of creation.

Furthermore, in the biblical tradition the more recent acts or events do not make out of date those which took place earlier. Even when the more recent are clearer or more remarkable. Precisely because the recent past or the present are not to be understood without reference to further back in the past. Or again because what is new is an unfolding of an expectation without which it would not have come to light. So it is that Jesus, the new Moses, does not cancel out the great leader of the Exodus. Any more than the Risen Christ diminishes the Jesus of Caper-

naum. And no more than the christology of St John renders obsolete
that of the synoptics.

That seems to me to explain what I call faith-memory. It is constituted as an unbroken movement from happening to happening, whether
going back in time or inversely following history as it unrolls, always
however in the continuity of mystery. In other words, the believing
memory is a universal process which far surpasses this or that particular
memorial. Certainly the memorial is indispensable. But it is so as a
witness. In it the memory makes present an aspect of the past. But it is
not concerned with this aspect only. What interests it is the universality,
the inner coherence, and the present power, of the time that is past.
For it is on these foundations that hope is made possible and that there
is reason to attend to the present.

In other words, by advocating a remembrance of baptism I do not
mean to introduce some peculiar novelty little known to christian
experience. I claim rather that there is a latent potential written into
the common programming of christian memory but too often left aside.

Baptism a dimension of faith

The baptism we have received has a time and a place in our past.
This means that the mystery of God in its universality is addressed to
us individually and has taken shape as an event in our lives. What God
wants for the world, what he brings about in and by his Church, this is
personalised for us in that act which made us christians.

And it is just because the mystery of God has been made event that
it can give rise in us to memory. Our baptism took place. But it could
not have been. It is inscribed in our history as a contingent act. It was
a sign set over our life so that we might be a gospel sign in our world.

This historical aspect is of first importance. It gives to christian
spirituality a concrete, personalised anchorhold. Just as in the Exodus
there was a founding event for Israel, just as in Jesus Christ there was a
foundational event giving birth to the Church, so there took place in
our life a moment we can consider as a foundation in faith. The gift
of God is for the baptised, therefore, not simply what might be glimpsed
or generally perceived in the heart, or on the borders of faith. It is
what happened one day to you. It is what took shape for you. The event
serves here as a pointer or land-mark for keeping the significance alive.

And this is why to make a remembrance of one's baptism is to keep
alive the power of the event. It is not merely to remind oneself that
faith is a gift or that the christian life is grace. It is to turn towards a
real though indistinguishable moment in our past. This could remain
psychologically a sort of empty formula with no fixed content. But even
so it is a sign. For even stripped bare the event continues to form us.

Calling baptism to mind

Lastly, we have to call to mind our baptism. In the strong sense of the word, 'inform' ourselves. For the aim is not to recall. It is to be increasingly more capable of memory. Therefore more and better baptised.

In fact, if we must indeed make a remembrance of baptism it is not merely for the pleasure of consciously entertaining a concrete symbol, one probably irreplaceable, of what God has worked in us. It is far more in order to set our baptism to work. Put another way, it is to start our faith-memory going.

For baptism is the gift of this memory, its inauguration, its beginning, and its formation in us. In the Holy Spirit the baptised are integrated into that immense believing tradition stored in the Bible and of which we still feel the power today. To be baptised is to believe — and to be able to believe — that past has still not said its last word. It is to take on oneself and into oneself the obligation and opportunity in that long sequence which is God coming to mankind and being manifested in Israel, in Christ, and finally in the Church and in the world.

Baptism in this sense is the sacrament of christian memory.

Memory and hope

It is not arbitrary to affirm this. It rests on the conditions in which baptism came to birth in Israel, carried by a popular prophetic movement the pioneers of which like John the Baptist were reaching out towards the end of time and the merciful forgiveness of God. Historically baptism is pre-christian. It took its rise in judaism, in the upsurge of hope during a period which was crushed and disillusioned. You might think that as a result it would turn its back on the memory, send it packing in favour of eschatological urgency. Actually a self-analysis such as this, so little conformed to the biblical mentality, takes no account of John the Baptist's message, nor subsequently of the message of Jesus.

For in fact John the Baptist does indeed signify the end of a world. It is a turning-point in history, a last-chance gesture, the final liberality of God. But it is still an act of memory. And that in a twofold sense. Firstly because hope in the divine forgiveness rests on what God has already brought about in his own: baptism in this sense completes but does not abolish. Next, because the baptised confessed their sins on entering the water of sanctification. In other words, they took up their past again, recognising that it was not in line with faith. Here we have another kind of faith-memory entering in. No longer one making present founding events but one which acknowledges before the face of God the misery of mankind.

I would say therefore that baptism, by the act in which it is born, shows that memory will save us if it has the well-spring of hope and if it has a part in conversion. To be baptised is to be given the possibility of such a memory. It is the recollection of tradition under a personalised form, directed to the future which God promises and the change in our life which he is awaiting.

In memory of Jesus Christ

Jesus' own baptism was like that: it was his enthroning before God and humanity, the point of his effective and decisive insertion into the memory, the hope, and the will to conversion, of his people.

Christian baptism is like that today: the saving entry into a historical tradition, the one Jesus assumed and which he has transmitted to us. So much so, that without losing its essential components of biblical tradition, hope, and conversion, the memory communicated in the act of baptism also includes for us, finally and supremely, the name of Jesus Christ. To receive christian baptism is to be given the biblical memory as John the Baptist had already set it going, and Jesus took to himself by his personal experiencing of it.

From now on it is christian baptism which can as such be considered as 'memorial' of the event and mystery of Jesus. Again it is necessary to see what exactly that implies.

The word 'memorial' is employed in contemporary theology above all for the eucharist. This is not by chance. Jesus' formula at the Last Supper as Luke gives it takes exactly this standpoint: "Do this as a memorial of me" (Lk 22,19). For the christian faith, the eucharistic action enters into the continuity of the Covenant, and makes present the action of Maundy Thursday fulfilled in the Easter resurrection. It is memorial because it is based on Jesus' initiative and on the action of God, because it refers at once to the mystery and to the event, because it is Christ's command handed down to christians, and because it is a definite celebration inserted in time so as to maintain a permanent faith-memory. I add in common with current theological expression that the eucharist does not repeat the event which it commemorates. It does not start it over again and is not to be numbered along with it. But it reactualises it, that is inserts it in time at another point from that of its historical manifestation. From this standpoint the eucharist does not repeat the Last Supper nor the Cross nor the Resurrection, but gives them new presence at the time they are celebrated.

Why is the eucharist the outstanding christian memorial? For two reasons. Because of Jesus' word at the Last Supper: "Do this in memorial of me", which is rendered more simply by "do this in memory of me". And also because the 'this' referred to concerns a decisive happening in the life of Jesus, the one in which he gathers up his whole life and gives it its ultimate meaning of gift and faithful love. In the eucharistic memorial therefore is a word of authority which invites us to commemorate an event and, because that event is an ultimate moment, communicates mystery.

What has this to do with baptism? In some sense the two factors characterising the eucharistic memorial are found again there. But they appear in rather different fashion which, as we shall see, makes of baptism a memorial somewhat distinct from that of the eucharist.

Baptismal memorial

Let us be clear first of all that the New Testament hands on to us a word of Jesus on baptism which has a certain analogy with that concerning the eucharist. On the evening of Maundy Thursday, Jesus had asked his own to do as he had done. After death, the Risen Christ confides to his disciples an ecclesial mission. And this mission includes baptism: "Go therefore and make disciples of all nations, baptising them in the name of the Father and of the Son and of the Holy Spirit" (Mt 28,19).

Nevertheless, beneath the parallelism of these two words of Jesus the differences are plain. Not only because in one case it is the historical Jesus who is speaking, while in the second it is the Risen Lord we hear. But especially because the commandment to baptise does not rest on a scene which Jesus asks to be re-enacted, as is the case with the eucharist.

Does this mean exactly that christian baptism does not go back to any historical point in the life of Jesus? It could certainly be referred to the baptism of Jesus in the Jordan. But supposing the evangelists to have tended to adopt this view and to see in the baptism received by Jesus "the foundational event behind christian baptism",[1] it remains that the one is not expressly given in the New Testament as making a remembrance of the other.[2]

Hence the query: Is it well-founded to speak of christian baptism in terms of memorial? I think so. But what this memorial makes present is not in the first place some point in the life of Jesus and in any case not primarily an inaugural moment, like the baptism

1. The expression is from M.-A. Chevallier, *Souffle de Dieu, Le Saint Esprit dans le Nouveau Testament*, Beauchesne, 1978, p. 122. This interpretation is not shared by all biblical scholars. The German exegete R. Schnackenburg, for example, maintains: "I am not convinced that, in the New Testament, the baptism of Christ is intended as relating to the baptism of the faithful" (in a joint work: *Les Sacrements d'initiation et les mystères sacrés*, Fayard, 1974, p. 153).
2. Liturgical and theological tradition has however widely commented on this connection.

in the Jordan. What baptism remembers is Christ's commitment taken as a whole. This is, besides, the very point of view of St Paul in Romans 6 when he links the Church's baptismal action with the death and resurrection of Christ.

Two sacramental 'memorials'

The question then takes another turn. How indeed avoid asking why there should exist in christianity two sacramental memorials, baptism and the eucharist, and what exactly is the distinction between the two? It could of course be replied, taking account of the fact: so it is, christianity is at once baptismal and eucharistic. But why so?

Let us note first of all that baptism leads to the eucharist. This is what happened for Jesus himself. He began his mission under the sign of baptism, in the place of baptism on the banks of the Jordan, and from there went on to the eucharist in the Upper Room. In other words, as the witness of Jesus himself indicates, we do not arrive in one bound at the eucharist, it is not the beginning of the gospel life. Jesus, who had undergone the rite of baptism, who recognised in this action the passionate eschatological urgency actuating it, finally instituted the sacrament of the Last Supper. As though to stress the full scope of baptism. As though to signify the lengths to which the hope and courage linked with baptism can go. On the evening of Maundy Thursday, Jesus does not disown his baptism, he makes a remembrance of it in function of his own experience and the death awaiting him.

Next, it is plain that baptism is a rite of entrance of inauguration. It marks a threshold. It is this also which ensured its standing in the hellenistic world as a kind of equivalent of jewish circumcision for the pagans. To be baptised was to enter the people of the new Covenant, be marked out as a member. Consequently baptism is not repeated. It takes place once and for all. It seals the passing from unbelief to faith. Next comes the eucharist. It is repeated continually. In one way it 'goes further' than baptism, for it allows entry gradually into communion with Jesus by making remembrance of what was most radical in him, the gift of himself. Baptism, as understood by Romans 6, is doubtless not closed to this significance. But it puts our oneness with Christ comprehensively and it is for the eucharist to 'cash' this bond by making remembrance of Holy Thursday and Easter.

We can thus understand why christianity is built around the two essential 'memorials'. Baptism and eucharist form one structure. They are not to be dissociated. But they stand apart. This separation indicates a road to travel and precisely an initiation to be realised. To be initiated into the christian faith is to go from baptism to eucharist, that is to say to take upon oneself sufficiently the baptismal action to grasp that it goes towards the eucharist and to be able to maintain the baptismal foundation of the eucharist without which it could not well display its full range.

Remembrance of Christ or remembrance of baptism?

Baptism is therefore a memorial. It is, like the eucharist, an act of remembrance. To baptise someone is to make a remembrance of Jesus and to stamp that remembrance on a being for it to be made that being's own.

But a difficulty remains. That the baptismal act provides us with a remembrance, right. But why direct that remembrance back to what makes it possible, to baptism? Why recall baptism when there is question of making remembrance of Jesus and his mystery? Is not wanting to make remembrance of one's baptism turning the remembrance back on itself, disorienting it in a sense, taking it improperly for an entity when it is at the service of mystery?

This sort of question requires taking a good look at to see what is in play. We are, obviously, not the centre of christianity, it is Christ who is that. But each time we go towards him, we go also towards ourselves. For his presence makes us persons and assures us of our own identity. There is consequently no conflict between making a remembrance of Christ and making a remembrance of baptism. For, by referring back to the baptism we have received, we are still looking to Christ but by celebrating what he has done for us individually. Our being there does not disturb his presence.

Rather, it contributes to its manifestation. In fact, the remembrance of our baptism adds to our relationship with Christ. It allows us to realise that Christ is really come in us and that gratuitously, with no possibility for us to take his coming as a matter of course. We might not have been baptised. That we are, leads us to value in our faith what it has of thanksgiving and praise.

Consequently to make remembrance of baptism is not to give way to the evil spirit of introversion. It is to believe in Jesus Christ as he was and as he continues to be for us.

*   *   *

About christian remembrance

Before closing this chapter I should like to emphasise and clarify what we have found concerning initiation to the christian faith:

— The whole of the consideration you have been reading is centred around the theme of memory. You will have remarked that a kind of inversion has occurred on the way. My first care was to reactivate baptism, to make of it an explicit object of our faith-memory. And so it is that, indeed, baptism appeared first of all as a source of memory. If therefore we can go back to it, it is because, at a deeper level, it enables us to do so.

— To define baptism in terms of memory is not usual, it is true. It is for the eucharist that contemporary theology reserves the term memorial. But this interpretation seems to me quite well founded. It rests on what we can learn of the baptist movement at the beginning of our era. It is authorised too by what the eucharist is. For it would be useless to want to give back to baptism its place in the christian experience if it could not be closely *correlated* with the sacrament of the Last Supper.

— Baptism reshapes the faith-memory to which it is the introduction. It is an act of tradition as well as of novelty. It means a leap of the believing memory, a decision aligned with hope and the certitude of divine forgiveness. This leap is basically experience of Jesus. So much so that we have been baptised in his name, that is to say into his experience and his memory.

— It is not without importance *in our day* to underline the importance of memory in christian initiation. At a time when tradition is disfigured by the efforts of some, or made ridiculous by the pretentions of others forgetful of the past, it seems to me an indispensable and salutary task. To be christian is to believe that the God of Abraham, Isaac and Jacob, of Moses and the prophets, has given himself in Jesus and that this long movement by God towards mankind is the world's authority for a grace-filled future.

— Finally, it has become apparent, exactly on a line with remembrance of Christ, that christian initiation has *two poles*, baptism and the eucharist. These two sacraments make present the same unique paschal mystery. But they do it in different ways. The one is celebrated once for all, the other enters regularly into church life. The one expresses the decisive advent of faith, the other manifests in Jesus Christ the significance of the Kingdom present in a human life.

3

You are become
what you were

A bi-polar initiation

You were baptised. You were confirmed and you have taken part in the eucharistic celebration.

That happened. That has stamped you.

But that is not ancient history. What you have received and what made you christian does not lie in the mists of days gone by.

In practice all this was a signal for you of progressive entry into the christian memory. That is to say into a salvation that you can live day by day in reference to Jesus Christ. Baptism has provided you with this possibility, confirmation ensured it in you, the eucharist set it to work. Thus you have been put in a position to become what you are. You were made and you are become christian.

The sequence of initiation presents itself therefore as much an entry into christian memory as an entry into the mystery of Christ. The two standpoints are equivalent.

But it is essential to distinguish in this sequence the two poles, the starting point and the finish, baptism and the eucharist. Two different ways of stressing the christian faith.

Baptism indeed marks the first beginnings of faith; it says this by its opening words and first stages. Whereas, the eucharist expresses the faith as the Last Supper expresses the experience of Jesus, that is to say in the maturity of an extended experience, which is yet capable of being condensed into a decisive act. It follows that some christians live the faith rather 'on the side of' baptism, where others experience rather the side of the eucharist.

A liking for beginnings

In practice, a baptismal outlook in christianity benefits faith at its outset. To be christian according to this perspective is to have the sense of always beginning in the faith and to feel continually taken by surprise at believing in the Gospel in a world ruled by indifference, where the christian message becomes commonplace in a well-worn routine and cheapened by the noisy media. Take good note, this way of being christian does not dissolve into the interminable indecisions of those

C

who cannot find their identity. To claim baptism is to recognise that a step has been taken and a decision has to be made. But a christianity lived with baptism as its dominant note spontaneously returns to that original moment of faith when gospel newness was not yet blurred and the pledge of conversion not yet gone to waste behind believing by habit.

It appears to me that such a perception, too little in evidence in christian communities one-sidedly focussed on the eucharist, seems very valuable in our day. Christians of this stamp are less people of doctrine or ceremonial than witnesses to something which has surprised them into life. Those around them notice in them the gospel paradox of power alongside weakness. They themselves are aware, by a kind of intuition of the heart, of the gropings and birthpangs of the faith in those who come their way. Perhaps also they are, without always consciously realising it, quite sensitive to what is implied by memorial in the christian faith. Their prayer is 'blessing', taking that in its jewish sense, which indicates a prayer making remembrance of God's benefits to mankind. Their christian responsibility seems to them to consist less in 'converting' the Church than in keeping alive the memory of Jesus Christ in the world.

By experience

Happy are we if we make a remembrance of Jesus at his beginning in us and if we turn towards him as to the one initiating, making a start.

It is paradoxical that we do not quite comprehend how things began until after the event. We do not know what it is to believe until after beginning to believe. By experience. It takes not less than the whole of christian initiation and then the whole of life to bring out in us the powerful effects of those first beginnings.

This was the conviction of the early Church. Baptism and eucharist were not spoken of except to those who had already been baptised and made their first communion. The new christians, if they were adults, spent the whole week after Easter in meditation on what had happened to them. This was the custom understood by the term 'mystagogia'. This distinctive name indicates a movement advancing towards mystery, that is to say the spiritual dynamic starting from the beginning which later becomes remembering or recapturing a lived experience.

Here is what Cyril, Bishop of Jerusalem in the 4th century, declared: "I have wanted for a long time to speak to you on these spiritual and heavenly mysteries. But, knowing that we trust to our eyes more than to our ears, I was waiting for the present time in order to find you more attentive as the result of experience . . . You are become able to receive more divine mysteries, now that you have been able to accept the divine and life-giving baptism. Therefore, since henceforth it is necessary to set the table and feed you with stronger food, well then I am going to give it to you with care so that you really know what happened in you on the night you were baptised".[1]

Here again is what Ambrose, Bishop of Milan, said on a similar occasion at the same period: "I am starting on the explanation of the sacraments which you have received. It was not fitting to give it earlier. In the christian, indeed, faith comes first".[2] Entering on the consideration of the meaning of biblical types of the sacraments of initiation, he points out: "If we had intended to allude to this before your baptism, when you were not yet initiated, our handing it on would have been thought to be a betrayal. Besides, the light of those mysteries is more penetrating in those who are not expecting it than if someone's words had gone before".[3]

Not saying too much before the ceremony so as to allow to the ceremony a role properly initiatory, not 'spoilt' by commentaries however well-intentioned then, later, coming back to what took place, so as to grasp its significance: this is true christian initiation. This return to the past constitutes a work of faith. It does not consist in an emotional recovery of feelings or impressions which are gone, but reactivating what will from then on give form to the life to be led.

Risk of emotionalising the spiritual

To make a remembrance of one's initiation is therefore not to multiply artificially images or reconstructions and family researches to find out 'how it all went'.

I am always struck at infant baptisms by the camera flashes popping. Parents, relations, friends, want to catch the moment, the event. And that is entirely understandable. But what will today's baptised think of if all in ten or twenty years' time? They will be faced with a trace of their past. They will have in front of them proof of what happened. But that will not dispense them from making remembrance of their baptism. For that is a question of something else. To make a remembrance of one's baptism is not to look at a photo or a film, it is to make an act of faith. Beyond the private aspects of the event — the baby's face peaceful or in tears, the names and the dress of the people standing round — there is a work of faith to be achieved. We have to see ourselves marked by what went on. What was done presupposes besides that the flow of memory should not be interrupted. From Jesus to the newly-

---

1. First Mystagogical Catechesis, 1. Notice the stress laid on baptism, principal pole of initiation. Yet the newly baptised had already made their communion.
2. Of the Sacraments, 1.1.
3. Of the Mysteries, 1.2.

baptised a transmission of signs has taken place, thanks to the memorial practised in the christian tradition. Starting with the baptised person become objectively christian, in principle of course, the line of faith requires to be continued and the action of memory prolonged.

Have you noticed that this way of recalling one's baptism is analogous in its degree to that we make when we recall Jesus? In both cases the remembrance is a construct. It is, fundamentally, short on detail. For that is not the most important thing. But it is rich in correlations. It is a connector. We do not force ourselves to remember the time past but entertain its present worth. Seeing that God does not cease willing to finish what he began.

Danger of sacramentalism

To reactivate christian initiation in one's life, therefore, inevitably includes a risk of emotionalism. On the understanding that initiation has in itself the means of bypassing this 'fleshly' temptation to lead on to a spiritual remembrance.

I should like to stress another danger: that of maximising the sacraments by taking them for entities detached from their context. The pastoral mystagogia of the 4th century already shows signs of this tendency. Today if we want to make remembrance of what made us christians we need to take care.

We have two practical means of avoiding sacramental inflation. First of all, to set the sacraments the whole time in the total context of initiation. What we have received and are holding in remembrance is not only baptism, confirmation, and the eucharist, it is also the word of the Gospel, and the living memory of other christians through their witness past and present. Next we should clearly realise what is the dynamic of initiation. It goes, certainly, from baptism to the eucharist. But this movement is only the institutional form of a much fuller course, since it is on the way to the end of time and God's eschatological forgiveness, in accordance with values inherent in the rite of baptism. In consequence the eucharist which, besides, has also an eschatological meaning, does not keep all the faith for itself. Any more than it centres on itself alone our initiation remembrance.

All this presupposes of course that initiation shows what a sacrament is with neither an emotional high point nor a terminus exhaustive of the faith-act.

Continuous remembrance

I have shown how in the course of initiation properly speaking, an act of remembrance is made, whether in linking the eucharist with baptism, or developing the values of baptism without allowing them to be absorbed into the eucharist action, or returning mystagogically over what has already happened, or whether, finally, being radically on our guard against emotional inflation or hypertrophy of the sacraments.

To make a remembrance of this initiation is to continue along the same way. For basically there is no break between initiation and what follows. The faith-memory making initiation real is in line with the faith which informs that initiation.

But it is not enough to suggest theoretical principles. We have need equally to seek out practical opportunities allowing us to reactivate the initiation of our faith.

In this connection I should like to repeat that the essential seems to me to be a matter of baptism, the baptismal dimension of faith. I do not deny that celebrations could be desirable, for Pentecost for example, or during confirmation of young people, allowing for reactivating the confirmation one has oneself received. Nor do I dispute there being sometimes an interest in returning to one's 'first communion', the one initiating into the eucharist, although the chance of emotionalising might then be quite formidable especially if there is no reference to baptism to assure the quality of that remembrance. But, all things being considered, it is indeed the baptismal side of our initiation which demands priority for reactualising today.

How is this to be done in practice?

Opportunities in the past

On this point it must be admitted that the early christians had many more opportunities for recalling their baptism than we have today. Visiting the baptismal fonts was not unusual in certain parts of France about a hundred years ago. In the same way from the end of Antiquity there developed in the West the custom of celebrating baptismal anniversaries either collectively or in private.[1] The movable date of Easter made baptisms, even those celebrated, as was the norm, on Easter Day, to fall on different days. This sometimes involved fixing on a common anniversary day, for example the Monday after Easter Week. Gradually the spread of infant baptism and its celebration on very different dates, along with the lessening of the sense of baptism, brought about the disappearance of this custom.

There were other practices formerly which allowed personal remem-

1. Here is the text of an ancient prayer dating probably from the 6th-7th centuries which gives very happy expression to the meaning of baptismal remembrance: "O God, whose providence leaves no fact of the past without its consequence nor any hope for the future without its object, grant lasting effect to the past event which we are commemorating, so that we may always firmly keep in our actions what we relive in our memory" (*Introduction à la liturgie*, Desclée, 1961, p. 367).

brance to be made of baptism. For example in the course of popular missions in the 17th century the preachers often introduced ceremonies of renewal of baptismal promises, similar to those now suggested in the rite of the Paschal Vigil. At that period, St John Eudes was one of those who laid great stress on the place of baptism in christian life. This is something which could well have an appeal for us if it is true that numbers of our contemporaries need to discover or rediscover the faith from its beginning, and quite apart from the eucharist. Another practice: the linen cloth used to dry the newly-baptised was taken home, the christening robe the child had worn was kept, or the candle which had been lit at the end of the ceremony.[1]

Elsewhere solemn Mass was formerly preceded by sprinkling with holy water (accompanied by the antiphon *Asperges me*). It was an opportunity to evoke baptism: its place is not filled by the recognition of our sinful state which now opens the celebration of the eucharist. In the same way, in private prayer and particularly at morning and night prayers, the sign of the cross and the Our Father could have a baptismal connotation. Did not St Augustine say that the Lord's Prayer has this value: "In it you will find, as it were, your daily baptism".[2]

Their baptism and our baptism

It appears to me that the most effective opportunity today is to be found in taking part in the baptism of others. Participation in a child's baptism or that of an adult can be a favourable time for rediscovering our own baptism. What is happening for another person today, happened for us yesterday.

In this connection should be mentioned instruction for baptism. Increasingly, christians a little aware of their baptism and what the baptismal rite means for the Church and the world, take a part in sessions with people wanting to have a newborn baby baptised. Christians with this kind of experience know its great value. To talk about baptism and what that implies is surely to express one's own faith and remembrance of baptism.

Let me add that the variety of forms the sacrament of baptism may take today contributes, for anyone sensitive to it, to deepening its immediacy. The baptism of a child speaks of the radical gratuitousness of God's gift. The baptism of an adult expresses this same gift and gratuitousness through human consciousness and free adherence. And the one helps to the understanding of the other.

1. Making one's 'solemn communion' (very popular in France from the 18th-20th centuries) had obvious baptismal significance: white dress, lighted candle, renewal of baptismal promises.
2. G. Morin, *Miscellanea Agostiniana*, Vatican Polyglot Press, 1930, 1.1.

Lent and the Paschal Vigil

A second opportunity for making remembrance of our baptism is offered each year by the celebration of the paschal mystery. I am thinking of course of the profession of faith at the Paschal Vigil. Its unusual character, under the form of question and answer, is a direct echo of the baptismal rite. This is all the more perceptible in that the rite of blessing the Easter water which precedes it, has allowed those present to remind themselves they have been baptised. And this is obviously all the clearer if the baptism of a child or adult is celebrated in this context, the most suitable setting for such a ceremony.

But the liturgy of the paschal mystery does not consist solely of the Paschal Vigil. It also includes Lent, that long period of preparation for Easter. It is usually given a penitential sense, and also in our day a sense of sharing, spiritual and financial. Perhaps it might be a good thing not to forget its catechumenal sense. Traditionally indeed it is during these weeks that adults conclude their preparation for baptism. And if there is a Lent for the adults already baptised, historically it is because Lent was introduced for those to be baptised. So much so that the invitation addressed to those who were going to be baptised was extended to the already baptised. Consequently, following its basic logic, Lent is a baptismal time before being a penitential period or a time for sharing. Christians are called to renew their baptismal life by joining in the course of life of the candidates for initiation in view of their approaching baptism.

This significance of Lent seems to me to make certain demands on us today.

First of all the penitential aspect of christian life, that which characterises the sacrament of penitence-reconciliation, ought to be closely linked with baptism. Which allows, at least partly, of ensuring against well-known deviations. Sacramental penance, as the early theologians sometimes said, is a 'second baptism'. It reactivates it. It affirms that the baptised who have had difficulty in living up to their baptism can make a fresh start and gain strength from God's forgiveness. Therefore it is neither excessively moralising nor interminably psychologising. The sacrament of penance is very definitely a memorial of baptism. And it is a memorial which quite normally is joined to those other memorials, Lent and the feast of Easter.

On the other hand, if Lent associates the baptised with the course undergone by the catechumens and renews the one group by the newness of the other, it is easy to see that one of these lines of influence is not sufficiently esteemed today. Penitential and baptismal, it has become in our day a time of sharing. And that is a good thing. But the holding in common to which the baptised are invited is not confined to the

financial aspect, however important that may be. For Lenten sharing
does not consist solely in giving what we have saved by regulating our
lives and our consumption. It extends also to the faith christians live by.
In solidarity with the catechumens moving towards the conclusion of
their christian initiation, in faithfulness to their own baptism reactivated by conversion and the sacrament of penance, the baptised are in a
position to live Lent as *a time when their faith can be communicated.*
By going out to meet those around them, christians or non-christians,
in what they experience spiritually. In the ordinary exchanges of everyday life, in listening and caring, in having the humble courage to dare
speak out their convictions and aspirations.

Sunday and the eucharist

Another opportunity for making a remembrance of baptism is given
us by the Sunday eucharistic liturgy.

One of the christian teachers of the 2nd century, Justin, presents us
with valuable indications on this point. In his first 'Apologia', after
having described the unfolding course of christian initiation, he adds:
"After that, later on, we continue to make a remembrance of these
things" (no. 67). The phrase points out that the things of initiation —
baptism and the eucharist — need to be made present by the believing
memory. The next part of the passage shows how this on-going initiation
is maintained. What is striking is that the eucharist is neither the sole
nor the first way of doing it. Justin brings out first of all the mutual
assistance afforded each other by the candidates for initiation, the sharing of goods: "Those well-off come to the help of those in need".
Next he points to prayer: "We bless the Creator of the universe through
his Son Jesus Christ and through the Holy Spirit". The Sunday
assembly comes only in third place. In other words, if it has a manifest
part to play in a remembrance of initiation, it is not to be detached from
christian life as a whole.

On the other hand, the eucharist as Justin shows it, is not all there is
to Sunday. This day has value not only by reason of the eucharistic
celebration but in the first place because it is a memorial-day. It makes
remembrance of creation and of Easter resurrection. On these two
counts it is fitted to make a remembrance of christian initiation, which
is re-creation and entry into the paschal mystery.

It appears to me useful in our day to stress a point of view very dear
to the early Church but much less plain to us. That is the significance
of the calendar, i.e. time unfolding, objectively and socially, independently of what we may feel about it. Any given day is already, on its
own account, a possibility for remembrance, whatever may be the
celebration fixed for it. That goes for Sundays, in the same way as for

the jewish sabbath. It is the case also for the time 'programmed' for Lent, annual meeting time for the baptised, past and to be. It is again the case for the feast of Easter, movable but regulated, when each year is made real what we are.

Doubtless you see how far off we are from understanding this. And yet I wonder if there is not something very valuable here. For us, the Mass is sometimes quite independent of the day on which it is celebrated. It stands by itself. And if it is on a Sunday, that does not have immediate significance for us. For the early christians on the contrary the remembrance value of Sunday was joined to the remembrance value of the sacrament.

In other words, for them Sunday meant something to help us bring our initiation back to mind. For we do not fix the date for it, it is there before us in a way, just as what was communicated to us of the mystery of the faith was there before we were. And on the other hand Sunday makes remembrance of the Christ of Easter and of creation. In it the two terms of reference are conjoined. And here we have an important feature of initiation. A person is initiated into the christian faith not only by being associated to Christ but also by being re-established by him as a part of creation, and fitted to proclaim it to the world.

The sacramental system a memorial

The third way of making a remembrance of baptism already received: the sacramental life.

I have been speaking of the eucharist. I have likewise taken up the case of the sacrament of penance-reconciliation in which the baptismal reference is obvious. It is possible to enlarge the perspective and consider the sacramental system as so many opportunities of putting the 'basic' sacramental initiation to work.[1] The juridical fact, which consists in linking the reception — which is to say the full celebration — of the sacraments to the baptised state, is an indication in its way of this vital logic. To be sacramentally married, receive the anointing of the sick, be sacramentally ordained a minister, goes back to something previous, to christian initiation. The requirements for sacramentality refer back to a common condition defined by baptism and communion.

Besides it is this essential common to all christians which is restated by the funeral liturgy when life is at an end. It does it precisely by invoking baptism. The sprinkling of water on the body has this significance. The dead person will not communicate again but leaves as a baptised person. And when the christian service of the dead is accompained by the eucharist it is indeed initiation re-expressed in its fulness.

---

1. One of the theological criteria by which sacrament may be defined is assuredly memorial: the expression is not to be used only of the eucharist.

The dead person's departure is under the sign of baptism but also in line with the eucharist which has characterised that person's life, and in the farewell communion gathers together those surrounding the body, now without visible life.

A memorial instituted as sacrament

In going through the sacraments I have not said much about confirmation. I would in fact like to give it a special place according to the viewpoint adopted here. In the catholic tradition at least, this sacrament makes remembrance of baptism in a very particular way. It is a quite unique memorial of baptism. Baptism is in fact the only sacramental action which brings in another celebration having as its chief purpose to make remembrance of it. In other words, confirmation is a memorial instituted as a sacrament. Whereas all the sacraments have reference to initiation and thus have the value of a memorial, without for all that being solely defined as such, in confirmation it is the memorial which is central and which is sacramentalised.

So then baptismal life does not consist solely in living as a baptised person and making a remembrance of baptism in the liturgical rites, in charity, and in prayer. It calls in at one point an actualisation of baptism, significant and characteristic.

I shall of course return to confirmation. For the moment it is enough to have noticed its exceptional position. If necessary it could on its own be read as an indication of the importance of the baptismal memorial in the christian life.

Daily remembrance

One last way of making remembrance of christian initiation: the one already underlined by Justin and which has a part in the actions of everyday life, without memorial properly speaking, but with the aim of living what has been received.

It is a matter basically of experiencing christian life in a certain way. A way which may be called baptismal. It is in fact for the christian a manner of perceiving the life which flows from baptism and which conversely allows a better understanding of the present reality of the sacrament.

How are we to characterise this relationship between everyday life and baptism? I spoke above of the taste for beginnings and being bold enough to dare. I would add to this awareness other features which we have evoked en route. First of all the art of keeping in one's heart what happened, for its secret to resound little by little. And then also hope in God, the conviction that he is loving and forgiving and that consequently our life is never at a dead-end. But all that is not a lasting possibility unless at certain times celebrations and explicit forms of memorial enter in to maintain and revive the baptismal sense.[1]

*   *   *

Summary

If I am to attempt to draw up an account of the basic ideas used in this chapter I would wish to include the following points:

— To live as a christian one must become what one is, or, put another way, take up what has been received. Initiation implies a *journey* of this sort: a person is made a christian and becomes one.

— What ensures the link between what one is and what one is to become in christian initiation is *faith-memory*. To be christian we must receive a memory and put it to work in the form of fidelity and renewal through hope.

— The programme of initiation is therefore not confined to the *sacraments*. It implies everything characteristic of christian remembrance. In particular it presupposes learning to look back on what has been lived, without for all that having an excessively emotional reaction to the moments being considered.

— The time for initiation is not endless. A point comes when it is declared *ended* according to the institutions of the Church. But this ending is not a break. Life goes on, continuing in the same way as before. The memory especially is always at work.

— Again, christian life should not be defined solely in function of the end of initiation, that is to say the eucharist. It needs to maintain within itself the original *baptismal dimension*. This dimension is of particular meaning for modern times.

1. I should like to mention in this light two practices assuredly very different yet which both give a sense of baptism. First, what christianity calls *religious life* in the institutional sense of the term: to live as a religious is to feel a call to 'radicalise' one's baptism. Next a celebration which takes place in contemporary charismatic groups which they call *'outpouring of the Spirit'*, after earlier using the inadequate expression 'baptism in the Spirit'. It is a ritual of imposition of hands which can only have the sense of reactivating the baptism once received, and which was of course a baptism in the Spirit.

4

When should initiation begin?

For you (probably) it was done very early

You have been baptised. And you were probably baptised as a child. That was it.

Oh, of course, no one is forced to be a christian. Neither juridically nor spiritually. To force people is not God's way.

But anyway you were started on christian initiation at a time when you were not asking anything yourself, since you were not at a stage to be sufficiently conscious of what was going on.[1]

This state of things can most often be interpreted in two almost opposing fashions.

Sometimes people are worried at this way of doing it and do not want it applied to others especially their children. For they consider it hardly compatible with freedom of conscience, with modern culture which puts the accent on each one's personal responsibility, finally with the gospel message which is a call to free conversion and a decision in faith.

Or conversely people are glad they have been baptised while still small because they see in this a sign of God's love, a love addressed to all whatever their level of consciousness or psychological abilities. They add that the fact of growing up as a baptised person has great importance. If baptism is efficacious, as the christian faith affirms, it must surely have some effect on a baptised infant as it grows up.

If we wish to avoid simplist emotive expressions or one-sided naivety it is doubtless not necessary to oppose overmuch these two ways of looking at things. For after all, are they really incompatible? It could well be that one may seem preferable to the other according to circumstances, and temperaments as well. But it is not obvious that casting anathemas on the position not adopted is the surest way of seeing the matter clearly.

1. The early christians did not speak of initiation, in the sense of a progression. When they used the word (about which they often had reservations, given its non-christian overtones) they kept it for the sacramental rite of baptism and for the catechesis which followed. Today the expression has taken on a wider sense and designates the whole of the periods, stages, and rites, which form christian faith from its first steps until it is put into operation eucharistically. Therefore I am asking: when should initiation begin? where the early Church would rather have said: when should initiation be conferred? when should baptism be given?

In any case for you it's done. For you, exceptions apart, baptism meant infant baptism. That was how you were baptised.

But my query remains: At what age should christian initiation begin? Or rather: Should christian initiation of children begin with the rite of baptism? and since this is the traditional practice in the Churches, what are the arguments for it?

Infant baptism
since the early days of the Church

One opening question which is often put, bears on the antiquity of infant baptism. On that point we can be fairly clear. This custom goes back certainly to the beginnings of the Church even if it was not necessarily general from that time on. That obviously does not resolve the problem. But it does invite us to ask how the early christians were able to justify their way of acting.

In the New Testament indeed it is not said plainly that newborn children were baptised. Family baptisms spoken of there and which are called baptisms 'of the whole house'[1] do not expressly mention the children. But several indications lead us to think that infant baptism was a possibility.

There is first of all the jewish custom of circumcision. If St Paul could establish a parallel in his letters between christian baptism and jewish circumcision,[2] it is hard to see how the christian rite of baptism was not performed on newborn children since they had been given circumcision.[3] Or Paul would then probably have remarked on the difference.

Besides this, when a non-Jew wanted to become a member of the jewish community at the beginning of our era, he was in principle circumcised, then took a ritual bath, a baptism. His sons also were circumcised and baptised, his wife and daughters receiving the baptism of purification. The head of the family therefore brought in his family with him. And the baptism of the children, then, was normal practice. We may think that these jewish customs influenced the practice of the first christians. Therefore baptism was normally given to the children at the same time as their parents. And the children born to christian parents too were eligible for baptism so as to be associated with the condition of their parents. That could have been the case even when one only of the parents professed the christian faith.[4]

I would add in the third place that the early Churches were highly

1. Acts 10; 16,13 and 31; 18,8; 1 Cor 1,16.
2. Gal 3,26-9; Rom 2,25-9; 4,1-12; Col 2,11; Eph 2,11-22.
3. Phil 3,2; Col 2,10-15.
4. Cf. 1 Cor 7,14; a text difficult of interpretation.

sensible of solidarity in the faith, indispensable for baptism to be given to beings without consciousness yet members of the human family. This possibly gave grounds for legitimising infant baptism.[1]

A fourth argument is sometimes put forward in this sense. But it appears to me hardly convincing. This is the attention Jesus showed to children. They had effective access to him. And they are thought of in the gospel as bearers of an experience which could well tutor adults. But the children we meet in the gospel narratives are not newborn infants. And above all, the spiritual values they exemplify are arguably not to the point in a study of baptism.

Altogether therefore it was likely and even normal for baptisms of newborn children to be celebrated from the earliest years of christianity. Without our being able to say whether this practice, which could not have caused any problems while in existence, was quite quickly made general, or whether it was in limited use for a time. Infants were certainly baptised in the 1st century. It is not possible to say further whether children just born were baptised.

Received practice

Nor in the following century is infant baptism explicitly attested. But indications still more precise than those already mentioned, in practice make its existence certain.[2]

A layman in Rome, Justin, writes around the year 150: "Many men and women now sixty or seventy years of age have been disciples of Christ since infancy". Is this a question of baptism, the celebration of which would in this way be attested for around the years 80-90? We cannot say entirely. But it is very likely. It is not easy to see how, for the early christians, it could have been possible to be considered disciples of Christ without receiving the mark of a disciple, baptism.

In the same sense there are to be found comparable expressions in the account of the martyrs. For example in the acts of the martyrdom of Polycarp, which took place in 167 in Asia Minor. The martyr declares, speaking of Christ, "Here are now twenty-six years that I have served him".

Finally around 180 in Lyons, Irenaeus writes that Jesus "comes to save all men". And he adds: "All those, I say, who are born again in him, infants and children, adolescents, adults and old people". The expression 'born again' has very probably here a baptismal sense. It is applied consequently to every age without exception, including the newly-born.

1. This is clear in the accounts of miracles performed by Jesus (Mk 5,21; 9,14 etc). It is equally in this sense that can be understood the curious custom of baptising the dead, spoken of in 1 Cor 15,29.
2. It does not seem to be to the purpose to give reference to the texts I am about to quote. You will find them in the collection of J.-C. Didier.

A practice become general and normal

It is from the 3rd century that evidences of infant baptism are at once plain and numerous. They are to be found in christian writings and also on funerary stones dedicated to children prematurely dead.

It then becomes obvious that infants were baptised throughout the regions where the Gospel had been preached: in Egypt (Origen), in North Africa (Tertullian, Cyprian), Rome (Hippolytus, numerous burial inscriptions).

Generally, it is a practice considered normal, to the extent that it forms part of the baptismal rite transcribed by Hippolytus: "First the children are to be baptised. All of them who can speak for themselves will speak. As for those who cannot, their parents or a member of their family will speak for them".

All the same, we do not know whether, in the 3rd century already, all christians had their children baptised. In christian families the children were not necessarily baptised at birth. But numbers of them were, and the custom was considered as established. Proof is that the christians who did question it felt bound to justify their point of view and defend it against what appeared to be accepted practice.

We can therefore say that infant baptism is of very ancient provenance and goes back to the beginning of the Church. While we do tend to speak a little too readily of tradition to designate quite recent customs, the word can here be employed quite safely.

Infant baptism disputable

Infant baptism was not only a founding tradition. It was also and at the same time a practice under discussion. And this second feature is no less important than the first if we want to understand what is involved.

It would be naive to suppose that the debate concerning infant baptism as it is today is something completely new. From the 3rd century, when the practice in question is plainly and widely attested, we can observe a need for explanations on the subject and to found its legitimacy theologically, spiritually, and pastorally. The situation resembles that of today: some hold that infants should be baptised as early as possible, others prefer to delay the sacrament.

Infant baptism makes sense

Let us begin with the first position, the more widespread it would appear, the one which considers infant baptism as normal. Between the 3rd and 6th centuries those who held this position were led to found it on reason. Not that it had any need to be justified. It seemed to many to be self-evident. But as it was sometimes questioned there had to be arguments in its defence.

— First argument: *that is how it is done and how it has always been done.* Origen in the 3rd century wrote: "The Church has received from the Apostles the tradition of giving baptism to even the youngest". With the assurance of his convictions he therefore derives the custom of infant baptism from the apostolic age. Nearly two centuries later Augustine will be of the same opinion. He declares: "What the universal Church holds, what has not been instituted by any Council, what has always been maintained, can only come from the apostolic tradition". Or again: "The custom of baptising infants which is that of our mother the Church must not be despised, nor considered as of little use, nor judged to be other than an apostolic tradition".

— Next, there could be invoked to justify infant baptism *the equality of all human beings before God.* That is particularly brought out by a bishop of North Africa, Cyprian, speaking in the name of the local assembly of bishops: "What is expressed by this is the divine and spiritual equality according to which all human beings are the same in stature and in age. It is in human eyes that there are differences of age and corporal development, not in God's eyes". In this regard some quote the text of Matthew 19,14: "Let the little ones come to me". This phrase has not, as such, a baptismal connotation. But from the 3rd century it has been invoked with reference to baptism.

— Elsewhere, *infant mortality*, then very high, intervened to motivate immediate baptism. People did not want to let infants depart without having received the water of baptism. Evidence of this are the numbers of tombstones noting the baptism of a sick child. For example this one from Rome and dating from the 3rd century: "Florentius had this epitaph made for his worthy son Apronianus who lived for one year nine months and five days, greatly beloved of his grandmother. She, seeing him close to death, begged of the Church that he should leave this world as one of the faithful".

— Finally, fourth argument, if we wait too long is there not a risk of postponing indefinitely the age for baptism and of not giving the child the *spiritual strengths* which could afford it help? Some adult christians did indeed tend to defer their own baptism. We can understand that, by this very fact, they would be reluctant to ask for the sacrament for their children. Here is how a bishop of the 4th century, Basil, reacted: "You hesitate? You temporise? You have been a catechumen since childhood and have not yet made your adherence to the truth? . . . Your whole life is going to pass away in testing. You are going to be making trial of yourself into old age. So when are you going to become a christian? When shall we be able to call you one of us?" It is not a question here, it is true, of the baptism of babies. But the doubt about adult baptism necessarily implies that of the admission of children to baptism. Besides, a text here and there explicitly gives as motivation for infant baptism what is needed to lead a christian life through childhood. For example this one, written by a bishop of the 4th century: "The circumcision of Christ at work in baptism should be given early on to the small child for his safety: on the one hand so that putting on Christ as a breastplate he shall not fear hostile demons; on the other hand so that he be not delivered over to false doctrine and become its prisoner".

Other considerations

However, from the 3rd century some christians or certain tendencies in the Church questioned the custom of baptising the newly-born.

Here again I should like to list the arguments put forward in support of their theory.

— First point to be raised: *baptism presupposes faith.* How can children be baptised since they cannot themselves ask for baptism nor express their faith? "Let them be at least able to ask for salvation so that it can be clearly seen that it is given only to those who ask it" (Tertullian). In view of this some therefore put off their baptism. Not necessarily to adulthood, however. In the 4th century Gregory Nazianzen counsels baptising children at three years of age: "They can then grasp something of the mystery and respond to it. Doubtless they do not understand well but an impression is made upon them". Other christians hold that the newborn are legitimately baptised because they are carried by the faith of their parents.

— A second argument against the baptism of newborn children is that *no one can see into the future.* The baby cannot commit itself and no one can be sure how it will turn out. This is what Tertullian says: "Having regard to the state, disposition, and age, it is more expedient to defer baptism than to give it immediately". He adds: "Why, except in cases of emergency, expose those presenting the child to great danger? They could die without being able to fulfil their promises. And if they live, the children may turn out badly and deceive their hopes". In the 4th and 5th centuries some held these reservations so strongly that they did not have their children baptised and these, becoming adolescents and adults, were in no hurry to ask for baptism. This hesitation was sometimes ambivalent: people feared certainly not keeping their word but also they were trying more or less to avoid the practical demands, moral and religious, of the christian life.

— Third argument offered by the opinion desirous of delaying baptism: *children are not sinners when they are born.* "There is a question frequently considered by the brethren", says Origen. "Children are baptised 'for the remission of sins'. What sins are these? When have

D

they been able to sin? How retain such a motive for infant baptism?"
At about the same period, Tertullian was asking: "Why must this age
of innocence be in haste to receive remission of sins?"

The question was plainly put. In a way it was really when the matter
of infant baptism was reopened that it was the more hotly debated.
Begun in the 3rd century, the debate was to last until the 5th.

Origen, who was on the side of infant baptism, employs an argument
very significant for sacramental theology: "If there were nothing requiring remission and forgiveness of sins in children, the grace of
baptism would seem to be superfluous". In other words: custom makes
law, and drives theology into accounting for the practice. How can we
speak of sin forgiven in the newborn? Origen thinks that 'birth-stains'
might be called sin: a sin borne by every human being "by the fact of
being born". All this, as can be seen, is not very plain. And it could
even be very questionable if this theological argument is masking some
confusion made between birth and sin, or again leads people to understand birth as an impure act.

A contemporary of Origen, Cyprian, had another point which was to
find great favour in christianity. The child, he says, being recently
born, has committed no fault. But "the sins which are forgiven 'in
baptism' are not his own", they are inherited sins, a state deriving from
his belonging to humanity. We can see emerging here, long before
Augustine, the subject of original sin.

At the beginning of the 5th century a theological school linked with
one of the decisive personalities of the period, Pelagius, proposed another interpretation again. Let us admit infant baptism, he considered,
since it is a received practice. But we will reinterpret it. Redefine infant
baptism independently of sin, stop saying it is forgiveness of sin.

It is in this context that Augustine took a strong stand. For him the
pelagian teaching was dangerous. It minimised the effects of baptism,
questioned the unrepeatability of the baptismal rite, misconceived the
actual solidarity of human beings in evil and in sin, as in faith. "In
children just born and not yet baptised we must see Adam. In the
newborn who are baptised and so reborn we must see Christ".[1] For
Augustine, infant baptism in its plenary sense is to be interpreted in line
with the theology of Cyprian. To characterise this theory, he popularised
the expression 'original sin'. There is only one baptism, he said, the
same for children and for adults. And the baptismal ceremony is one
of the signs of God's gift offered to all and not even conditional on the
degree of consciousness in the one receiving it.

— A fourth argument advanced against immediate baptism of the

1. Sermon 174.

newly-born flows if you like from what I have pointed out in the first place. Little children are not capable of believing, given their age. If they are said to be fit for baptism it is therefore that they are carried by the faith of those who present them, and this family solidarity allows them to be enrolled in a certain sense in the number of the faithful. But one bishop posed his colleague Augustine a very practical pastoral question: what is to be done if the parents ask for the baptism with a faith apparently and very probably insufficient? You see how this type of question is not only from our day.

Here is Augustine's reply: "Do not worry that some, when they present their children for baptism, do not do so believing that they will be reborn in the grace of the Holy Spirit to life eternal, but thinking it to be a remedy to preserve them or return them to health". The reason for this recommendation not to worry in the face of superstition is this: "The child is presented not so much by those carrying it in their arms — although it certainly is so by them as well, when they are truly believers — as by the whole assembly of the saints and faithful". Consequently, adds Augustine, "It is then Mother Church entire who is working, she who is in the saints. The Church entire is constituted by all. As a whole she brings forth each one". It had been some time since anyone had explained this peculiarity of infant baptism: adults speak in the name of the child. Here is Augustine broadening the perspective. And it is starting from his considerations that the theological formula has become general according to which 'a person is being baptised in the faith of the Church'.

*   *   *

First statement of accounts

To what point had christian consideration of infant baptism arrived towards the end of Antiquity, in effect the 5th century?

It appears to me the following points can be drawn from the debate:

— The practice of infant baptism was *accepted*. Certainly it was sometimes challenged afresh. But opposition was in fact less widespread than the customary practice.

— We do not have the impression that christian parents felt *obliged* to have their children baptised. In any case no official text lays on them this obligation. The bishops contented themselves with defending the legitimacy of baptism and on the other hand inviting adult catechumens not to delay indefinitely their request for baptism.

— Infant baptism was continued but it served also to start up a *theological debate*.

— Whether conferred on the newly-born or on adults, baptism is a sacrament of *faith*. On this point there is no doubt. But that supposes in the case of babies that the concept of faith implied in the ceremony must be widened: it is the faith of the parents, of those attending, and finally of the whole Church.

As the practice of baptising the newly-born plainly shows, baptism brings in the question of *solidarity* in the faith. But that does not apply only to little children borne by the faith of the whole Church. It must *also* be found, in another way, in the case of adults. To confess one's own faith is no obstacle to doing it in common with other believers.

— Baptism of the newly-born is symptomatic of a kind of conflict of *allegiances* in the child. Family solidarity in the event widens into solidarity in the faith, extending to the whole ecclesial body. But this positive solidarity stands in opposition to another relationship, this time paradoxical and alienating, not unifying but divisive, that of sinners, of sin. Can we speak exactly of solidarity in sin? Probably not. But there certainly is a connivance, a compromise, among us sinners. And sin presents itself in our life as a kind of force weighing us down before we even consent to it.

— Baptism is a gift from God. To call infant baptism into question for greater psychological verity and spiritual logic, would have seemed in the first centuries of the Church to attack the *gratuitousness of baptism*. Baptism of the newly-born was thought of as one of the main signs of divine favour, it being also understood that God's love was attested in life and in the Church in many other ways.

— Baptism is a *memorial of creation*. It does not give entrance into any world other than that of creation. It does not introduce into a supernatural state outside of created reality. But it strengthens our relationship with the world. We are baptised, Justin said in the 2nd century, "so that we should not remain children of blind necessity and ignorance but should be children of true freedom and knowledge".

— Baptism conferred on children as on adults is the sign of *human equality*. It assimilates human beings not only beyond the level of consciousness where they are not yet conscious, but also beyond their differences of race, mental development, social condition. Among the baptised are neither Jews nor Greeks, freemen nor slaves, adults nor children, mentally handicapped nor geniuses. Children of the human race, we are born with differences and divergences. Becoming children of God, we are born again as children of God-given equality.

— Baptism is *forgiveness* from God. It is not only that, however. At the end of the 4th century, John Chrysostom insists on this to restore the balance of a theology which was tending perhaps to polarise too much on the sin inherited by the newborn. "You have seen how the benefits of baptism abound? And to think that many say its sole benefit is remission of sins". It remains, none the less, that any baptism, including that of children, has a connection with sin.

— The early christians well knew that children were not personally sinners. And yet they thought that infant baptism must, like that of adults, have reference to sin. Hence the idea of a *state of sin* which affects the newborn quite apart from their consciousness or responsibility. This is what has been called original sin.

— There is only a single baptism. It is unthinkable that there should be one given to adults (expressing forgiveness of sin) and another to be for children (and which would only be entrance into the eternal Kingdom).

— But if there is only a single baptism it was an advantage and normal for there to be *several ways* of performing the baptismal action. In other words the early christians approved the two aspects of baptism: adult baptism and infant baptism. Each of these accents different facets of the same unique mystery. Eventually there were to appear certain tensions between the two. An example: when in the 4th and even the 5th centuries adult baptisms were celebrated at Easter and Pentecost, for the children there was the tendency to celebrate baptism either a week after birth (by analogy with circumcision) or straight away (to insist on baptism as superior to circumcision).

— Infant baptism could be considered in the early centuries of the Church as *normal without being obligatory*.

— In the Church of the first centuries *differing* points of view on infant baptism were conceivable without seeing in this diversity a threat to unity. We are rather far from that understanding.

— In the Church at its origin there was less argument on the legitimacy of infant baptism than on its *opportuneness*. Even for those christians reserved in regard to the practice it was not a matter of saying that baptism for the newly-born was unthinkable or unjustifiable. But they wondered about what is implied and entailed in fact.

— Some among the christians of the early centuries *deferred* baptism, that of their children, sometimes their own. Their situation was rather different from ours. Today it is rather the ministers of the Church who suggest to some asking for baptism to defer it until they discover or rediscover the faith. But we do still sometimes meet catechumens who hesitate, do not feel themselves ready for the sacrament, or else are afraid to enter the Church as it is.

5

Ten centuries of practice
in christian initiation

A historical view of the Middle Ages

In the 5th century the thinking aroused by infant baptism had spread widely. The adult catechumenate had for its part organised initiation into the Church and taken over its significance.

In actual fact the following centuries leant on this combination of practice and theology. And we continue to rely on it. But still, new things sprang up meanwhile. The most outstanding factor was the rapid disappearance of the catechumenate, the Church baptising almost only children. Less important but full of consequence was equally the rise of sacramental theology.

The great turning point was however the Renaissance and the Reformation.

Consequently I should like to notice for the moment the evolution of christian initiation from the end of Antiquity to the beginning of the modern era, therefore from the 6th to the 15th centuries. But let me straight away point out that this is in fact western history, the Churches of the Near East and the Orient not having known any very marked developments or polemic in this area.

What therefore happened regarding christian initiation during the centuries between Augustine and Luther?

Changes in ritual

First of all infant baptism became in effect the sole form of baptism practised in the Church. For gradually adults were no longer baptised. The colourful scenes of the baptism of Clovis or barbarian tribes indicate the peak but also the approaching end of the high period of adult baptism. From then on it was mainly children who were baptised. The Church was become christendom.

This had for consequence a modification of the ritual. Until then the celebration of baptism was thought of as being for adults and was developed according to stages and symbolic actions which the system of catechumenate preserved and linked together. When the baptised came to be usually children there was an attempt at first to maintain the arrangement as it was. The parents were invited to take part themselves in the various liturgical stages provided by the catechumenate course. But they hardly ever did. It seemed an unsatisfactory solution. Gradually the rite for baptism shortened the intervals between the various ceremonies undergone by adults. In the 10th to the 11th centuries infant baptism came to have a condensed form of the adult ritual. This was the custom which remained in force until the recent liturgical reform, which moreover has not cancelled out the historical heritage: in fact, it is on the plan of the baptism ceremony for adults that the other baptismal rituals have been constructed.

For the present the reworking of rituals for the purpose of infant baptism entailed a modification in the length of time taken over the celebration and the ceremony itself.

Towards the end of the Middle Ages, baptisteries, freestanding buildings separate from the church, were exchanged for what were called 'baptismal fonts' sited within the church. The processions of earlier times between the baptistery and the eucharistic space appeared less meaningful once the baptised were newborn children. Further, the baptism which formerly had been given by immersion was more frequently performed by pouring the water over the child's head. This way of acting was considered more convenient. Finally from the 8th century, probably for baptism ceremonies in emergency cases which were therefore simplified, a new baptismal formula began to appear replacing the former questions and answers on the faith. It was a formula spoken by the priest alone, in his own name: "I baptise thee". As on the symbolic level the candidate for baptism became less important, there resulted added significance for the one baptising.

The 'indexing' of the ritual for infant baptism along with that for adult baptism had the advantage of maintaining the principle of one single baptism, whatever the age of those to be baptised. It also indicated that adult baptism remained in a way the norm. Somewhat curiously there continued to be a reference to the time for baptism being Easter Day or Pentecost although infant baptism was celebrated at any time throughout the year. But adapting the rite of adult baptism to infant baptism did not proceed without difficulty. The logical order of the catechumenate even when revised and corrected was not necessarily that called for by infant baptism. For a long time the arrangement remained a poor compromise. It was necessary to await our contemporary period for a distinction to be made between the two baptismal rites, one for adults, one for children.

Initiation continuing to be in stages

However, even though the act of baptism proper was condensed into a single celebration, christian initiation kept its stages.

First of all, confirmation, the rite performed by the bishop over the new christians, came to be set apart from baptism. That was because the bishop was not present at the ceremony when the newly-born were baptised. Besides there had been this custom in outline in the earlier period, for the same reason.

Next, first communion was cut off progressively from baptism. Until the 11th to the 12th centuries children who were baptised received communion at once under an adapted form similar to that still in use in the Eastern Churches. The newly-born were therefore baptised and communicated in the same ceremony. In the 12th to the 13th centuries communion was set later for them.

Two reasons for this change may be found. Firstly the development of eucharistic doctrine aroused very great respect for the communion rite. Sometimes moreover excessively so. It was therefore fitting to wait until the children were older to admit them to the sacrament. This resulted in a certain christian mentality. When 'everybody' is christian in theory, baptism is normal and to be done quickly, but communion becomes the sacrament to be received consciously and with discernment.

Initiation no longer what it was

That infant baptism became more general had a second consequence, that of an *inversion of the initiation process*. In the adult catechumenate, time was taken for the neophytes to learn to believe, to discover the Scriptures and to make their own ecclesial profession of faith, before receiving baptism. From now on, for children, the order is changed. The rite of baptism comes first whatever the preparation undergone by the parents.

We may then raise the question of catechesis after baptism. This was very plainly stressed by a local Council of Paris in the 9th century: "In the Holy Church of God at its origin no one was admitted to receive holy baptism who had not been instructed beforehand on the sacrament of faith and on baptism. But as in our day the faith is everywhere held in honour and as children born to christian parents receive the holy gifts of baptism before attaining the use of reason, it is necessary for them to take pains to learn, once they have reached the age of reason, what at a tender age they were incapable of".

This way of acting was not without foundation. It could be based on the practice of the early Church, which preferred for the rites of baptism and the eucharist not to give detailed explanations until after the ceremony. With the idea that adults could not fully comprehend the final stage of their initiation until they had been through it. This is what was called 'mystagogia', i.e. relying on the sacramental mysteries, and a conviction that they could not become objects of catechesis until after having been experienced in the celebration. What had been done for adult initiation could therefore be transferred to initiation of children. With one difference however. For the children, it was the whole process of initiation which henceforth followed after the sacramental rite. There was therefore considerable inversion of the original analysis.

Besides, there resulted a certain want of baptismal sense in christian and church life. People had been baptised when quite small, they wanted baptism and were anxious not to have to wait for it. But in fact remembrance of baptism had little enough place in christian experience.[1] The practice of individual or private confession which spread in the West between the 6th and the 10th centuries lent itself in course of time to taking over from the sacrament of baptism and its insufficient presence. Formerly communal and annual, now personalised and at scattered intervals, the sacrament of penance took on the function of the ancient catechumenate: discovery of God's forgiveness, learning a minimum of religious knowledge (the person going to confession had to recite the Creed and the Our Father). In other words, sacramental penance, once termed a kind of 'second baptism' became one of the main practical forms of baptismal remembrance. And from that fact it took on an important place in christian initiation even though traditionally it did not have that significance. This is a notable fact. So then, initiation into christianity can be rearranged, taking into account needs and circumstances. Its form remains the same but its progression and emphases may vary.

Efficaciousness of baptism

The history of baptism during the Middle Ages in the West presents another factor which was also to have many consequences. It is the insistence on the efficacy and in practice on the *urgent* need of the baptismal rite.

I have just said that in a christian age the eucharist has more prominence than baptism. And I remarked that the importance given to the eucharist in the Middle Ages had led to deferring children's first communion so that they might communicate with respect and understanding. Is all this in opposition to what I am pointing out now, which touches on the essential and indispensable recognition of baptism? I do not think so. The Middle Ages in Europe believed in baptising children without delay, therefore at birth, even going sometimes as far

---

1. There was however a 'minimum' of baptismal remembrance: people kept the anniversary of their baptism, went on pilgrimage to the place where they had been baptised, the parents carefully stored away their children's christening robe, etc.

as penalising negligent parents and asking people other than priests to baptise in cases of emergency. In that sense therefore this period was far from minimising baptism. But at the same time, the more baptism was held to be an urgent rite not to be superseded, the less place it had in the rest of life. It gave entry into gospel salvation, not lasting shape to christian living.[1] It was other sacraments, the eucharist and penance, which characterised the course of christian life.

Fundamentally, we inherit that idea. Baptism is looked on by many christians and people at a little distance from the Church as an indispensable rite for signing a newborn child. It is part of family tradition and what is owed to the baby. But afterwards christian life in the future is scarcely thought of as baptismal even by practising christians. Everything goes on as though baptism were living on its reputation. It exhausts all its significance at once and once for all.

In the Middle Ages the emphasis on baptism doubtless expressed faith in God's gift, confidence in the promise of the Kingdom. But as baptism was in practice always a rite performed for children, childish characteristics were transferred to it and coloured its sense. However much conversion to the Gospel may be a new birth, a baby's coming into the world gave to it a directly human base. While yet unbaptised the infant was considered incomplete. Its first birth was not enough to admit it to God's world. Furthermore, infant mortality, very high during the Middle Ages, prompted speedy baptism for the newly-born. The sacrament was a way of being forearmed against a continual danger of possible death. Lastly, the doctrine of original sin implied that the rite of baptism should not be deferred. To baptise newborn children was not only to complete in them their creation but likewise to withdraw them from complicity in that state of sin which could not fail to affect them by reason of their coming into the world.[2]

An obligation
not an unconditional necessity

I would add that for the christians of the Middle Ages, baptism was the sole and unique means of entering into relations with the God of the Gospel and the Kingdom. Outside of baptism no salvation. At that time there was no question of enquiring how God could 'love the pagans' and bring non-baptised persons into his Kingdom. His way of

1. It is strange to note that the word 'initiation' used in the 4th–5th centuries was practically not in use at all in the Middle Ages.

2. There has sometimes been emphasis in historical studies on a kind of inversion of the doubts marking out this period as compared with the earlier period. For Augustine the practice of infant baptism had been an argument in favour of belief in original sin. Henceforth it is this belief which conversely motivates or supports the practice where there appeared a need to justify it.

loving the pagans was to lead them to become christians. And that was a concrete possibility, for in those centuries the Gospel appeared spread world-wide and the Church seemed everywhere present. The offer of baptism had the appearance therefore of being open to all. For priests moveover this possibility was accompanied by the duty of baptising sick children at the earliest opportunity. Everybody, including babies of course, could and should receive baptism.

Supposing, so ran the argument in the schools, that a child of nature living in the woods was not baptised, God, they said, would have recourse in his regard to exceptional means, either by making him know the essential truths of the faith miraculously or by sending him in unexpected fashion a preacher or even an angel. This most clearly shows the normal understanding of baptism. The proposed exception confirmed the rule according to which baptism is the normal way to be delivered from sin and attain salvation from God.

However, the importance and therefore the urgency of baptism should not give rise to hasty practices. Medieval theology and in particular the teaching of St Thomas Aquinas insisted on this. St Thomas in his 'Summa Theologica'[1] proposed three precise and significant cases. First of all, he thinks, children cannot be baptised against the will of their parents. This was concerning Jews particularly. Consequently, the necessity for baptism in effect gives way to family solidarity. Or to put it rather better, there is no necessity for the baptism of the newly-born except in so far as the babies are truly able to be inserted into the faith of the Church.[2] In the second place, the Summa Theologica invokes the case of difficult confinements: "Children in the womb can in no way be baptised." Here eagerness to baptise would go against the corporal reality of the act: one person cannot be baptised on the body of another. Finally, St Thomas approached the question of the mentally handicapped. They are, he says, able to be baptised in the faith of the Church except if becoming adults and showing a degree of reason they have not shown any desire to receive baptism. Again, this commonsense rider marks the limits necessarily found in any generalisation of infant baptism. The urgency and obligation are not unconditional.

Difficulties sometimes

However, the indispensability of baptism for the newly-born met with a certain amount of opposition in the Middle Ages. These reservations, although fairly marginal, were a continuation of questions raised by

1. Question 68, art. 10,11 and 12.
2. Such was equally the advice of Pope Innocent III in 1201: "It is contrary to the christian religion to constrain a person to accept and observe christianity, whose will is constantly contrary and entirely opposed to it".

infant baptism in the early Church. They are nevertheless significant, given that this practice was henceforth almost unanimously received and widely justified theologically. Even in this context difficulties remained, therefore. Throughout christian history they are to be felt to a certain extent even when hardly recognised.

For the time being the debate, in certain circles noticeably affected by Catharism, bore on the absence of reason in small children presented for baptism.[1] What could their faith be like? An old question, a classic, if you like. But it surfaced afresh as though the theological arguments were not sufficient to settle questions which were not only of principle. In any case augustinian theology and its reference to the faith of the Church were again to the fore in the 12th to the 13th centuries.

I include here a simple example of this classic position: "You are not going to tell me there is no faith in this child whose mother has given him her own, wrapping it up for him in the sacrament until he is capable of receiving it pure and without wrappings, that is, able to understand it and therefore to acquiesce. Is the cloth cut so close that it cannot cover at the same time mother and child? Great is the faith of the Church. Will it be less than that of the canaanite woman who showed hers to be enough for herself and for her daughter since it was said to her: "Woman, great is your faith, be it done according as you desire". This passage is from St Bernard.[2]

*   *   *

Account of ten centuries

Let us check off the points before starting on the period of the Renaissance and the Reformation. What is the understanding of baptism for children between the 6th and 16th centuries in the West?

— It is an *accepted fact*. From this point of view these ten centuries continue the practice of the earlier age, spreading and establishing it with greater precision, pastoral and juridical. By degrees an obligation is laid on the parents to present their children for baptism within a given time. And from the 13th to the 14th centuries it was said: "The soonest possible".[3] As for priests, they were invited to baptise sick

1. Another objection referred to the actual rite of water. In the 11th–12th centuries the Bogomils refused baptism because the matter, the water, appeared exclusive of faith.
2. Sermon 66.
3. In Latin 'quamprimum'. The word was used by the Council of Florence in 1441.

children immediately. The shortened ritual adopted for baptism by the Middle Ages was likewise entirely suited to a ceremony considered to be urgent. And it is probably in this context that from the 8th century the baptismal formula 'I baptise thee' replaced the ancient rite of question and answer on the confession of faith. However if there was a medieval tendency to emphasise the role of the minister in the baptismal action as in the other sacraments, it must be said that in the opposite sense emergency baptism led to authorising other persons besides the priests to celebrate baptism. From this angle baptism is not so 'clericalised' as the eucharist, which in the carolingian period became more and more the office of the clergy performed before a more or less passive congregation.

From the theological viewpoint the Middle Ages thought of infant baptism along the lines of earlier considerations and more precisely in *continuity with augustianian theology*. Newborn children are capable of baptism in the faith of the Church given that they form part of the christian faithful, a solidarity normally mediated by their family, and given also their solidarity with a sinful world in which they take up their place. Perhaps it should be said that the gift of forgiveness which baptism effects is sometimes at this period emphasised almost as though it exhausted the whole of the meaning of baptism.[1] But the Councils and theology usually kept the balance, spiritual and doctrinal, by a reminder that the action of baptism has also a positive effect, the gift of divine grace.[2] From this same viewpoint, desirous of avoiding the excesses of a schematised and vulgarised augustinianism, thomist theology reminds us that the faith of the Church, into which the newly-born are baptised, does not remain as an entity unsusceptible of concrete mediation. The children are not to be baptised unless their parents ask for it.

— One difference from the early Church: the western Middle Ages thought of *baptism as in fact possible for all human beings*. This the early christians did not say. Certainly they held that a person could not be saved without the rite of baptism. But for them the Gospel was not yet preached to all. Whereas medieval man was convinced it was. However, medieval christianity left two openings to what was later to become

1. For example the profession of faith demanded of the Vaudois by Pope Innocent III in 1208 declares: "We believe that, in baptism, all sins are forgiven". And in 1439 the Council of Florence, in a decree drawn up to prepare the way for union with the armenian christians affirms: "The effect of this sacrament is the remission of all sin, original and actual, as also of all pain due to sin".

2. The Council of Vienna, in 1312, affirms — with reference to the theologians — that baptism is not only forgiveness of sins but also a gift of grace. Likewise the Council of Florence balances the formula quoted in the preceding note with this one: the baptised "are withdrawn from the power of the devil and adopted among the sons of God".

the theology of salvation for the non-baptised. There was first the hypothetical case of the child of the woods. Then there was, much more concretely, that of Jews living among christians.

— Another difference from the previous period: in the Middle Ages *infant baptism became in fact the sole form of baptismal celebration.* Adult baptism practically disappeared. This had for consequence: the ritual was modified and the process of initiation inverted. In addition it led to considering baptism in the human context on the basis of early infancy. It was less often realised from then on what the sacrament of new birth might have to say to an adult. Baptism continued to be called the first of the sacraments but it characterised the ordinary course of life less than the eucharist or sacramental penance.

— Even allowable and allowed, infant baptism none the less kept a *paradoxical aspect.* Two indications show this in the medieval context. First the tendency to keep something of the pastoral guide-lines adopted earlier for adult baptism, notably concerning the date of the celebration. This was traditionally tied to the feasts of Easter or of Pentecost. However, reference to these appears to have been increasingly a formality. In fact, baptism was given as early as possible, i.e. on almost any day. What equally evinces the intrinisic difficulty found in baptism of the newborn is the renewed questioning of this practice which continued to arise here and there, sporadically it is true.

— Finally it must be noted that western christianity had occasion to think of the christianity of the East in the matter of baptism. For example the eastern christians baptise using a formula traditional to them: "N. is baptised in the name of the Father and of the Son and of the Holy Spirit". The passive voice reproduces the language of the Bible and emphasises the primary action of God. Priests in the West said, from the 8th to the 9th centuries practically: "I baptise thee . . .". Without exaggerating the difference between the two expressions, we can at least see that they did not present the role of the priest in the baptismal action in the same way.

On the other hand eastern christians did not habitually baptise straight after the birth. They adopted symbolic intervals: the eighth day by analogy with jewish circumcision, the fortieth or even the eightieth day to await the churching of the mother. Western christians found these practices suspect of judaisation. They appeared surprising to them, not bowing to the systematic haste advocated in their own Church.[1]

---

1. Conversely, the Orthodox Churches could not fail to find it surprising that in a case of emergency a non-baptised westerner might validly baptise a child, on condition of wanting to do as the Church does. This custom appears in the West from the 7th century.

Another difference, less marked: the eastern churches had not adopted in place of immersion the custom of pouring the water over the head of the child being baptised. Now, this had become the ordinary practice in the West by the end of the Middle Ages.

Further, for the eastern churches, giving the sacraments to little children was not restricted to baptism. The newly born received at the same time the anointing with oil —— which was called 'confirmation' in the West from the 5th century — and communion, under the form of a little consecrated bread or wine. The West had a different practice. Confirmation, reserved to the bishop, was normally given several years after baptism.[1] In addition, from the beginning of the 13th century communion for children was put back to the age of reason,[2] but always after confirmation. We see therefore a pope of the 14th century protesting against the idea that the validity of infant baptism could be tied to their reception at the same time of the eucharist.[3] A good indication, assuredly, of difficulties of comprehension between East and West.

Finally, there was a certain theological divide between the two types of christianity. Since the 12th century, the West had developed a sacramental theology of which the East, less given to precision and uniformity in the sacramental system, had not felt the need. Besides, the accent in the West on original sin and the place given to this dogma in the thinking on infant baptism had no equivalent in the East. There resulted a certain amount of difficulty. Thus it was that a pope of the 14th century, writing to the patriarch of the Armenians, was surprised to see the doctrine of original sin little appreciated by his correspondent, forgetting that it manifestly bore the western imprint of St Augustine.

---

1. A small fact indicative of the misunderstanding between Churches: in the 8th century at the start of the separation between western and eastern christianity, Pope Nicholas I affirmed that the greek custom of having the post-baptismal anointing (what the West called confirmation) conferred by a priest and not the bishop, was invalid.
2. Fourth Council of the Lateran, 1215.
4. Benedict XII, 1341.

6

Christian initiation
from the Renaissance to the 20th century

The Renaissance and the Reformation

The 16th century marks a turning point for the western history of infant baptism. The problems raised by this practice and which we have found latent in the Middle Ages again become manifest. But this resurgence is in a new form. We do not at first hear the baptismal tradition again put in question, but there was a desire to redefine its pastoral and theological conditions. In other words, instead of augustinian theology, now become generally accepted, being repeated, it was used along with its accretions as a starting point and there was a search to verify whether the way of celebrating baptism for the newly-born answered to the demands of the christian faith.[1]

The chief witness to this attitude is obviously Luther. But he was not alone in wanting a fresh study of baptismal practice.

So it was that Erasmus insisted on freedom for children to have the the possibility when they were of age of ratifying the baptism conferred on them. Basically he proposes what was later from the 17th century to be called the 'profession of faith'.

But the time for this solution was not yet ripe. It gave the impression of minimising the rite of baptism and its full significance. It was related to what many people mean today when they say that a child shall 'choose later on'. Erasmus had no following. A text of the Theological Faculty, then the Sorbonne, significantly expresses the official reaction of the religious authorities: "This counsel which suggests asking baptised children, when they have reached adulthood, whether they confirm what their godparents have promised in their name at baptism, and in case they do not confirm it, to leave them to their way of thinking until they repent, and that they should not otherwise be punished than by refusing them the sacraments of the Church, this is an impious counsel".

The reasons for disavowing Erasmus are next indicated. First, there is the danger of seeing the children abandon christianity. Next, this proposition increases the liberty of the individual for, it is said, in every

1. The word 'initiation', absent from the medieval vocabulary, reappears in the 16th century.

society and in all religions children are submitted to the heritage and religious obligations imposed on them by adults. Two motives that for us appear less obvious than they were at that time. The Council of Trent in any case would ratify this position.[1]

Erasmus' proposition appears noteworthy to me. however. For it evinces an outlook that was fairly new. Humanism considered infant baptism as putting in question the child's freedom of conscience. It was inspired, not in the first place by the possibility of the child being counted a believer by right of the faith of the Church, but rather by his existential humanity. Where Luther would advocate a revision of baptismal practice in the name of gospel faith, Erasmus moves in the same direction in the name of man and his freedom. And he proposes, actually from a point of view familiar to augustinian theology, to give a twofold aspect to liberty by distinguishing its fundamental constitution, where baptism can operate, and its conscious exercise, where adherence by the individual is indispensable. This anthropological view is often invoked today in debating infant baptism.

Baptism again central

Erasmus gives his proposal therefore psychological and cultural motivation. At the same period, Luther would be adopting a more biblical and theological direction.

His doctrine is along classical lines. He insists on faith without which baptism of the newborn is a piece of magic, and on the word of God which the baptismal rite manifests as efficacious. "If there is no faith, baptism serves for nothing. It is even harmful".[2] But, he adds, "my faith does not make baptism, it receives it".[3] For "baptism is not just water. It is a water made up of the word and the commandment of God and thereby sanctified in such a way that it is divine water: not that baptismal water is in itself more noble than ordinary water but because the word and the commandment of God join with it".[4]

Luther therefore accepts the practice of infant baptism. But with certain conditions which are those of every act of faith.

It seems to him that baptism must again be centred upon the gift of God, instead of being understood one-sidedly from the human viewpoint. It is an action of the divine Word before being a safeguard or a necessity for man. The difference is not simply a subtlety. It leads to speaking of faith not merely in terms of the human aspect or of ecclesial solidarity but in terms of adherence to the Divine Word and, more

1. Session 7. canon 14.
2. Of the Babylonian Captivity of the Church, 1520.
3. Great Catechism, 1529.
4. Ibid.

exactly, to the promise it bears. "Baptism justifies no one and is of use to no one. What justifies is faith in the Word of promise to which baptism is conjoined".[1] Original sin is therefore a secondary motivation for baptism. What is primary is response to the divine command and confidence in God's promise. Luther loves to quote in this connection the text of Matthew 28 ('Baptise all nations') and Matthew 19 ('Let the little children come unto me').

Reforms of the rite

What in practice are the consequences of this 'baptismal theocentrism'? They came to light in the time of Luther and after him.

The Reformation intended first of all to make the celebration again central by suppressing from the baptismal ritual everything added by 'the invention of man': the rite of salt, that of the oil, the signs of the cross, the candle rite, the white vestment, etc.[2]

At the same time it sought to restore greater liturgical verity to baptism. The baptismal promises were suppressed, seeing that the child could not make them for itself and that those presenting the child could not answer for it in this matter. The adults would, admittedly, continue to give an undertaking. But it would be for their own part and not in the name of the child.

This liturgical piece of improvement made it possible to avoid inept interpretations of the faith of the Church into which a newborn child is baptised. And for the first time in western history a difference of ritual was introduced for adult baptism and for infant baptism.

Two other distinctions further allowed the Lutheran reformed movement to return baptism and its celebration to their fundamenal significance.

Firstly, the celebration of baptism had to take place in the framework of an *assembly* and ordinarily in a *service of worship*. Here we have an attempt to 'reclericalise' baptism after the emphasis on individuals, privatisation indeed, which it had known in the Middle Ages.

Again, the Reformed Churches emphasised that baptism should not normally be conferred except *by a minister* of the Church. This is a way of reacting against the medieval tendency to 'urge' its celebration even to accepting that baptism might be given by a non-christian. It is also a manner of insisting on the connection of the baptismal rite with the Word of which the minister is the qualified testimony. Finally it was a practical means of making the celebration 'more liturgical'. Neverthe-

1. Babylonian Captivity, 11.
2. However, "it was the Lutherans who were the most conservative; the Reformers of Strasbourg and the Zwinglians were more so than the Calvinists and the Anglicans" (von Allmen).

less, this norm of baptism celebrated by a minister had not the same force in all the Churches issuing from the Reformation. If the Reformers are unyielding on this point, the Lutherans maintained in practice the medieval usage, which is still the catholic one in urgent cases.

Baptismal remembrance

Finally, the Reformation gave prominence to what could be called 'post-baptism'. Since the newborn child is baptised without being able to intervene personally in the act which opens to it the Kingdom of Heaven and makes it a member of the Church, let it at least later on live by this sacrament which gives direction to its existence. Luther does not make his own the suggestion of Erasmus. It advantaged human experience too much for him to integrate it into his theological and pastoral thinking. But he is anxious for the baptised to take up their baptism.

This was to be first of all thanks to catechesis. The importance Luther gave to the catechism with examination or yearly testing, with a view to participation in the eucharist, is very clear. The Reformer himself drew up catechetical works. I will merely remark that he was not properly speaking the inventor of the catechism. The word appears in the 14th century. In the 15th century Gerson and Archbishop Antonine of Florence published simple manuals of christian doctrine. But it was in the 16th century that the effort became widespread, profiting by the invention of printing. At the same time as Luther, catholics like Canisius and Robert Bellarmine produced catechisms, and the Council of Trent required a general exposition of the catholic faith to be drawn up, which was published in 1566.

Secondly, the Reform movement undertook to restore to christian living the *remembrance* of baptism. Luther himself insisted on this: "The sacrament of baptism, even the sign itself, is not the matter of a moment, it has a lasting significance. Although the celebration is soon over, the thing which is signified lasts until death and beyond: until the resurrection, the Last Day. For as long as we live we do what baptism signifies: we die and we rise again".[1] Here again, this is not entirely new. While allowing baptism to become above all a means of salvation leading on to the eucharist and the life of faith, the Middle Ages was not entirely ignorant of baptismal remembrance. But the Reformation emphasised still more the enduring dimension which baptism gives to christian life.

---

1. Of the Babylonian Captivity of the Church, 1520. The text adds: "You have once been sacramentally baptised but you ought continually to be baptised by faith".

However, and this is a third feature, it was not a question for Luther properly speaking of confirming baptism, especially if the *confirmation* in question was considered as another sacrament distinct from it. Confirmation could certainly be celebrated as a blessing. But it was not sacramental as it did not have reference to a saying of Christ and was not matched by an explicit divine promise. Without these two conditions there was for Luther no sacrament properly speaking. For him in consequence christian sacramentalism polarised into baptism and the eucharist, with the understanding that confession referred back to baptism constituted a very valuable celebration: "Penance is nothing other than a return to baptism, taking up again the work begun and abandoned".[1]

Consequences of the Reformation
Baptism recentralised as it was presented by the Lutheran movement had consequences which still persist.

The first of these consequences was the acknowledgement that baptism *unites* christians with one another at a profound level whatever the divergencies otherwise separating them. In actual fact the divisions between catholics and the reformed effectively did not occur on account of the doctrine or practice of baptism but because of other problems, touching notably on the eucharist and the role of ordained ministers. Basically the divisions among western christians in the 16th century marks the final step in the medieval period of putting greater emphasis on communion than on baptism. The baptism ceremony counted certainly but was inaugural and it was the practice of christian living, in particular the eucharist, its conditions and significance, over which there was dispute. But in the event baptism remained the bond of unity.

At least in the 16th century. For later on the heated polemic contributed to bring on opposition concerning mutual recognition of each other's baptism in the separated Churches and Confessions. It was necessary to wait until the 20th century for ecumenism to rediscover baptismal unity: a person is not rebaptised who has once been baptised into the christian faith and who wants to change Church allegiance or ecclesial community.

Second consequence: the impact of the Reform was considerable and it had as a reaction important effects in the Catholic Church with what is called the Counter-Reformation. The question of initiation was to be marked notably by the stress laid on the *institutional church*.

Called to consider the theological and pastoral disputes between catholics and the reformed, the Council of Trent dealt with baptism in its 7th session in 1547. It did not make a detailed study but limited itself

---

1. Great Catechism, 1529.

to considering the principal points of difficulty. Some of these went back to the medieval debate. So it is that the Council defends against manichaeist tendencies the value of the material element, which is the water in the baptismal ceremony. But the essential point was those matters in dispute at that time. Infant baptism was declared legitimate and definitive. It was made clear that the sacrament of baptism celebrated by the reformed christians is a 'true baptism'. There was insistence also on the practical effects of baptism. The sacrament does not eliminate sin entirely in the life of christians, and on the other hands it leads them to live not only in the faith but according to the laws of the Church.[1] Further, baptism is to be confirmed. For the Council, confirmation is 'a veritable sacrament' not a simple 'ceremonial' as the Reform would have it.[2]

Where does freedom come in?

The most characteristic feature to my mind is what touches on freewill. Erasmus had posed the question in line with humanism and Luther had developed it from the gospel viewpoint. The Council of Trent could not evade the question. On the one hand, it said, baptism is necessary for salvation. It is not then a free decision in the facultative sense. On the other hand a person who has been baptised cannot go back on what was done. Infidelity does not annul the baptismal state and children baptised at birth cannot properly speaking decide later on whether or not to ratify their baptism as Erasmus wanted. Finally the Council emphasises the ecclesial aspect of baptismal life. Baptism introduces a person into the Church and consequently obliges to respect of her norms. The baptismal commitment is not renegotiable. Besides, the Council does not see, despite protestant reservations, any difficulty in speaking of the baptismal 'promise'. That did not seem to go contrary to either the child's freedom or the radical and total gift of God. It even adds that the basic direction imparted to a life by baptism can branch off later to other vows.

It can be seen that the theology of Trent lacks something of the new positions whether humanist or reformed. The Council is above all reacting to protestantism. But it speaks of freedom without understanding what the Reform meant by fighting for a more evangelical baptism

1. Curiously, Trent employs the vocabulary of initiation for the 'stages' of the priestly ministry. The fact is symptomatic: it is ministry which becomes the point to which initiation refers when the sacraments of initiation no longer suffice.
2. There was no question at the Council of revision of the ritual. This would have conceded the claims of the Reform which the Council was not prepared to do. Therefore there were henceforth in the West several forms of baptismal celebration: those of the Reformed movement and that of the Catholic Church.

celebration and a christian life more closely centred on God's gift. What Trent says subscribes to traditional ecclesial logic but is not open to the sensitivity beginning to appear at the time.[1]

Infant baptism again

The Reformation's undertaking had a third consequence. It led some of its adherents to bring up again the very legitimacy of infant baptism. This, in spite of the lively opposition of Luther and Calvin. Certain of the Reformed, considering baptism as a sacrament of the faith, denied the augustinian theology, and in order the better to honour their evangelical tenets, refused to baptised the newly-born, and began rebaptising adults who came to them after having been baptised as catholics while still small. They were called 'anabaptists' (ana : again).

Luther argued against this attitude and way of acting. And that in the name of doctrine itself: "We ask God to give him the faith. Nevertheless it is not for that reason that we baptise but because God has ordained it". He adds: "Thanks to the prayer of the Church, which offers the child and which believes — and all things are possible to prayer — the infant is changed by the faith communicated to it".[2]

The polemic was heated. Never except on very rare occasions[3] had anyone been rebaptised in the Middle Ages. But anabaptism went further than the unaccustomed practice. In fact, it intended to restore primacy to adult baptism. In this sense it still bears witness by the present forms of baptism to a useful reminder: the baptismal type is adult baptism.

Revival of baptism

The history of infant baptism taken further forward by the Reformation was to know at the end of the 16th century and during the 17th century a resurgence, not only in the Churches of the Reform but also in the Catholic Church. Was there here, indirectly, a certain protestant influence on catholicism? It is likely. In any case, the 'internal' needs of the catholic communities explain this phenomenon, at the same time as does the doctrinal synthesis of the Council of Trent.

1. The Middle Ages in the West had opened up a little — only a little it is true — to Eastern christianity. Trent marks the end of this difficult beginning. From then on the western problem was concerned with national cultures. The influence of the East did not make itself felt again until towards the end of the 19th century.
2. Babylonian Captivity, 11.
3. Of the Flagellants, notably.
4. The Council of Trent had, besides, not altogether forgotten it. In the conciliar texts on justification, a little before those on baptism, an analysis of conversion is given in terms of adults. But adult baptism itself remained theoretical.

If we study this point by reference to events in France we can see that the revival of baptism took several forms. There was first of all stress laid on the catechism, for children[1] and also for adults, the latter being invited to attend parish missions. Within the framework of these missions a second element developed: christians were invited to make a remembrance of their baptism and to revitalise their faith and religious knowledge by reference to the sacrament once received.[2] After Borromeo had instituted in Italy the renewal of baptismal promises, John Eudes and then Grignion de Montfort, in the 17th and the beginning of the 18th centuries, suggested similar celebrations in France. At the same period, Bourdoise and then Vincent de Paul and the Priests of the Mission developed the practice now become typically French of solemn communion, at which children or adolescents who had completed the basic cycle of the catechesis renewed their baptismal promises.

Problems and trial experiments

Thus was brought about the connection between the development of the catechism and that of the parish missions, or again between the pastoral care of children and that of adults. But this association was not without its drawbacks.

First of all because the baptismal remembrance became a stage — the last — in initiation, rather than a possibility for adult life. In effect the 'renovation', whose connection with confirmation was in any case not very plain, was aimed at the children and lost at a stroke its significance for all christians as a whole. It was an initiation rite, not a memorial rite.

Next because baptism was reactivated as a promise. Without entering here into the difficult debate on this term, which the Reform opposed and Trent had retained, we may at least regret that the baptismal remembrance was reduced to a single aspect which implied an evident danger of moralism or voluntarism.

Finally, because the reference to baptism celebrated in the framework of solemn communion risked being submerged by the eucharistic

1. Following on the catechism of the Council of Trent (1566) and the works of Bellarmine (1597–8), the catechisms of the French bishops only began to appear towards the end of the 17th century: that of Cardinal Fleury (1679), that of Bossuet (1687). The development fanned out very quickly: for example the catechism of J.-B. de la Salle (1703) and also the imperial catechism drawn up on the orders of Napoleon (1806).

2. The catechisms supported this venture. For example, the catechism drawn up after the Council of Trent: "They will not fail to recall the obligations towards God which each one contracts on the day of baptism". Or again: "These truths . . . should be made the object of the continual thought and care of those christians who would remain faithful to their baptismal promises, so solemn and so sacred".

event. The eucharist certainly has the value of baptismal remembrance. It completes baptism. But in a church with but little sense of baptism as a lasting action, the eucharist easily tends to occupy the whole sacramental field. In fact this is not exactly what happened, or at least not in what is called popular christianity. Solemn communion and the renovation of baptismal promises have never achieved a very clear link. In French public opinion, the 'renovation' held great prestige for a long time and even a kind of autonomy. This is doubtless a sign that in France the eucharist is not the whole of christianity. Today in an age when the faith needs to become baptismal again and even catechumenal, before being eucharistic, it is not therefore surprising that the two elements moved apart. The 'festivals of faith' which have taken over from the former renovation ceremonies (but more often without much reference to baptism) are not always necessarily eucharistic.

Catechism and renewal of baptism: to these two forms of the revival of baptism must be added a continued effort on the part of the clergy, in the 17th century, to keep infant baptism as early as possible. A heritage from the Middle Ages, this practice was warmly defended at that time. For many it was one of the essential signs of belonging to the Church, on a par with the Sunday observance.[1] For Tridentine christianity it was this that expressed the strength of its cohesion and its convictions.

Adult baptism again a fact

The period of the 16th and 17th centuries knew another important fact regarding baptism, but one beyond the confines of the old christian countries. Missionaries were preaching the gospel in Latin America, India, China, Japan, and for the first time for centuries adult baptism became again a reality in the Church. Still more than the anabaptists of the Reformation had done, the catholic missions resumed an ancient practice.

The Council of Trent had not really taken the missionary situation into account. It had been created by the discovery of the New World. But the fact was there. Profiting from colonial administration, the gospel preachers baptised en masse and with speed, most often with a minimum of preparation. It was a matter of simple catechesis. But from the middle of the 16th century in Mexico or in Goa, a beginning was made on giving some sort of organisation to the period of a few weeks leading up to baptism, introducing rites from the catechumenate and even, in the Jesuit missions in Goa, devising a period of 'retreat' in a 'catechumenate house'. Not much valued in America, where care was

1. An ordinance of Louis XIV in 1698 required that all children should be baptised within twenty-four hours of birth.

rather for implementing the Council of Trent and its directives, the idea of a catechumenate made its way in India and in China, and at Rome, where a cardinal of the pontifical curia, Sanctorius or Santori, drew up a ritual for a catechumenate in stages. This work, based on research into ancient documents, was composed between 1578 and 1602. It never became official but it influenced certain missions in the 17th century, particularly in China. It is therefore in the 16th and the 17th centuries that the adult catechumenate reappeared in the Latin Church: a remarkable facet of the revival of baptism in this period.

This revival found symbolic expression in the ritual for baptism published in 1614 by Pope Paul V, included in a complete Roman ritual. It was the first time that the rites of baptism had been fixed for the whole Catholic Church. The text took note of the customs then current. Alongside these it gave a ritual for adults which repeated and adapted more or less the baptism ceremony for infants and proceeded with distinct stages, without therefore a catechumenal perspective properly speaking, and a ritual for children taking up again the various historical accretions. This ritual was to remain in force for three and a half centuries, until 1969.

A dormant period

If the 16th and 17th centuries constituted a high period for baptism it has to be said that in the two following centuries it knew a certain obscurity.

In the 18th century the revival was maintained at first. Grignion de Montfort was busy with it and the French episcopate were careful to see that baptisms were celebrated at birth. Initiation courses were organised for children already baptised, with catechesis, first communion, confirmation, solemn communion and renewal of baptismal promises.[1] The age at which this last stage was celebrated tended to be later: the solemn communion was hardly ever made before the age of 11–12 years. But the Revolution was to unsettle this pastoral work. The storm overthrew accepted customs. In 1792 the Church in France saw itself disestablished. From then on, the baptismal register was no longer the same as the register of births. The secular link between coming into the world and the sacrament was therefore no longer so evident as before. Besides, the criticisms made by Voltaire and the encyclopedists against infant baptism found an echo, if not in behaviour, at least in people's thinking. Finally the refractory priests did not recognise the acts of the constitutional priests and in several regions it was a new anabaptism that

1. In the 18th century the word 'initiation', again in use in the 16th century, begins to designate not only baptism proper but the whole process of christian formation.

was developing, to the extent that children baptised by the official clergy were rebaptised.

All this did not prevent baptism in the 19th century from remaining a solid fact in France. However, there was an unmistakable indication of troubles to come: the interval between birth and baptism plainly grew longer. In other words, the eagerness of the Middle Ages was no longer current and episcopal fulminations could do nothing against the new ways gradually gaining ground. The reduction in infant mortality and migration from the country into the towns explains this change of habits. But there is more to it than this. A certain amount of discord developed between the clergy and the christian public. The moralising authoritarianism of the Church over baptism as in other areas[1] and the upheavals of the industrial revolution had an immediate effect on baptismal practice.

In the face of this situation catholic pastoral work continued with what it had been in the habit of doing, catechism and parish missions. One factor however was new, the tendency to set back the age of confirmation. It was a way of maintaining a stage to be attained at the end of the catechism course other than by solemn communion and the renovation. For confirmation continued to be before this final celebration.

Another initiative developed towards the end of the 19th century, outside Europe. Cardinal Lavigerie instituted the catechumenate in Africa, with progressive stages and lasting several years. It was doubtless not without precedent since the catechumenate had existed since the 17th century in the Chinese missions. But it was a considerable advance on what the previous period had undertaken.

*   *   *

Summary

What from the point of view of christian initiation should be retained from the four centuries between the Renaissance and our era?

First of all there was adopted fairly explicitly the view of a need for *initiation*. In other words it was not only baptism which was under consideration in theological debate and pastoral work.

1. For example the famous Mortara affair in Italy, in 1858. The public authority carried off a little jewish boy a maid had baptised unknown to his parents. This was done in the name of the church authorities who considered the child christian and that he must be brought up as such.

— In this perspective the problems of catechesis, liturgy and still more of a *baptismal remembrance* became considerable.

— But christian initiation found it hard to write into its programme the *changes* of outlook characterising the West in the 18th to 19th centuries. Faith-memory was not able to react sufficiently to the cultural changes of the period.

7

Christian initiation
in the 20th century

Christian initiation re-examined

With the 20th century we again have beginning a period with strong feelings about initiation.

The first years of the century were important for catholics. In 1910 Pius X required that holy communion, until then celebrated for the first time in life around 11–12 years of age, should enter earlier into a child's life. This led quite often to changing the traditional order of the sacraments of initiation, confirmation staying linked to a relatively mature age and therefore occurring usually later than first communion. Thereupon the problem arose of knowing what exactly this sacrament effected. The more so as, since the 19th century, people had become aware of the unity in christian initiation: as is shown by the rapid adoption of this term, from before the last war and again at Vatican II.

Around the nineteen-fifties the problem widened. Once again people began discussing infant baptism, its meaning and legitimacy. At the same time the question of adult initiation presented itself, no longer in distant countries but now in Europe itself.

I do not want to retrace this history in detail. I would rather take one aspect of these considerations, particularly clear as much among protestant christians as among catholics, that of baptism of newborn children. Without forgetting to include in relation to it the other debates christian initiation is arousing today.

On what conditions should the newly-born be baptised?

Among protestant, before the last world war, Karl Barth, inviting christians to be more 'confessing' and rejecting a church looking more to numbers than to standards, opposed the practice of baptising the newly-born. A great debate ensued between 1950 and 1960, at once pastoral, historical and theological. In France in 1951 was introduced a liturgy of 'presentation' of children to God and the Church, with a view to baptism later. At the same time was reaffirmed the legitimacy of immediate baptism of newborn children. The 'presentation', corresponding to what catholics call 'reception', reinstituted therefore a succession of stages in the baptismal process for children.

In the Catholic Church the question is often posed in more guarded terms. In 1951 the French episcopate recalled that "parents (have) a strict duty to ask for baptism for their children" and that "as early as possible". They say specifically: "the fact that the parents are not practising does not allow us to number them among the apostates. The outward advance made by the parents in asking for baptism is a presumption in favour of their religious intent". All the same the passage suggests a kind of objective criterion: "If the children already in the family have been denied a christian education, baptism will not be granted unless there is a promise of sending the child presented for baptism to catechism classes in due course, and in the first place the older children as far as is possible".

In 1964 the Second Vatical Council promulgated the constitution 'Lumen Gentium'. This text does not deal expressly with infant baptism.[1] But it has played a part in the catholic thinking of the past few years. First of all Vatical II insists on the 'necessity' of faith and baptism, and therefore of the Church, for all those who have an understanding of these.[2] Next the Council takes care to spell out the various meanings of baptism. If the rite of baptism regenerates by incorporating into Christ and by giving entry to his divine fiiliation, equally it admits into the Church.[3] In this, Vatican II follows in the line of tradition, but consonant also with contemporary sensitivity, very aware of the ecclesial bearing of the sacrament. Elsewhere the Council reminds us that baptism is only a beginning. That is to say it calls for a sequel, a life of faith and witness. This implies also that it does not always lead on to the same ecclesial interpretations in all the various Churches and christian communities.[4] Finally Vatican II takes under consideration the restoration of the ancient catechumenate as it had developed in Latin America, China and Algeria, then, after the war, in France. It speaks of christian initiation for adults[5] and requires the revision of the baptismal rite provided for them,[6] which was done in 1974.

In 1965 a new intervention of the French episcopate sought to go further than the text of 1951. In a note intended for the priests,[7] the

1. But the 'Constitution on the Liturgy' a little earlier asks for a revision of the rite of infant baptism to adapt it to the factual condition of the newly-born and to develop the role and the responsibilities of the parents and godparents (no. 67).
2. Lumen Gentium, no. 14.
3. Ibid. no. 11, or no. 7.
4. Decree on ecumenism, nos. 3 and 22. Cf also Decree on the missionary activity of the Church, nos. 11 and 36.
5. Decree on the missionary activity of the Church, no. 14.
6. Constitution on the Liturgy, no. 66.
7. It will be noticed that this document makes no reference to christian lay participation in the baptismal ministry of the Church (for example in instruction for the sacrament).

bishops envisage more plainly than they had done hitherto a veritable pastoral ministry to parents who ask for their child to be baptised. Baptism enters "into the entire mission of the Church", that is to say it is bound up with the preaching of the faith and church membership: "The sacrament of salvation, baptism is necessarily a sacrament of church membership". The pastoral goal consists in giving parents "the means of exercising their responsibilities", by ruling out in their regard "both harshness misconceived as zeal, and mistakenly tolerant compromise". In practice the bishops propose "something of an interval between registering the child, which can be done before the birth, and the celebration of baptism". During this time of 'accompanying' can take place "meetings drawing their inspiration from the catechumenate".

Something of an interval

This suggestion is important from several points of view. For the first time since the Middle Ages, it ties in infant baptism with the catechumenate standpoint. As I have emphasised, attempts formerly made to bring the parents themselves to go through something of a catechumenate had scarcely any success. The problem is to know whether today in another context 'preparation for baptism' stands a better chance. At present it often appears quite useful, the more so as it profits in public estimation from the similar work undertaken in preparation for marriage. But it is obviously only in the longer term that the results can be judged.

On the other hand the institution of an interval between the first application and the ceremony allows emphasis to be placed on the decision on the part of the parents and of the minister. "The indispensable decision as to whether or not to confer baptism will enter in at the proper time". The actual text: "If some parents, after a time of reflection, do not want to have their child baptised or would prefer the baptism to be deferred, the priest will respect their decision but at the same time he will have a care, highly mindful of pastoral charity, to remain in relations with them. Baptism is not *refused* by the Church: *though delayed, it is still desired by her*".

New perspectives?

In 1969 appeared the new Roman Ritual of Infant Baptism as Vatican II had desired. Three features characterise the text. First, the official reintroduction of a scripture reading into the ceremony. Next it is no longer as though the baby was invited to make the act of faith. The parents, godfather and godmother, speak in their own name. Finally the ritual suppresses or makes optional certain ceremonies judged secondary or as overloading the main rites: the salt of reception, an anointing with oil which was until now performed before the rite of water, and the formulas called 'exorcisms' intended to keep from the child the spirit of evil.

But this ritual obviously did not settle the problems of the baptismal pastorate. Hence the third intervention of the French episcopate in 1971. In fact the text of 1965 suggested arranging for an interval between the request for baptism and the ceremony. Here and there some priests and christian communities had gone further and interpreted this recommendation along the lines of a children's catechumenate or again a 'baptism by stages'. This was for parents of little faith and for parents who, while themselves living the faith, wanted their children to be allowed to take a personal part in the final act of their baptism in due time.

Meeting at Lourdes, the French bishops recalled first of all their approbation of infant baptism: "It is not for us a matter of discipline however venerable. It is an act of faith in the absolute gratuitousness of the always prevenient love of God". Then they gave encouragement to the 'pastoral of accompaniment' which was presented in 1965. But there is no question in their text of a 'baptism by stages'. The formula, which might risk opposition to infant baptism, was not retained. Perhaps also it appeared to be too quick off the mark, given that the starting of a progression in stages would require a pastoral scheme for which neither public opinion nor even the catechetical organisation were prepared. A final point from the 1971 text: if the practice of immediate baptism remains the norm, there can be 'exceptions', in other words cases where baptism can be deferred and that particularly "in certain christian sectors".[1]

Initiation as a whole

Since 1972, it appears to me, the question of baptism has altered noticeably, especially in France. I mean that the problem of infant baptism has entered gradually into a wider context, that of initiation to the faith.

I take as proof of this several convergent indications.

First of all, the adult catechumenate restored in France after the second world war and recognised officially by Vatican II came gradually to be acceptable and to acquire a certain amount of influence. In 1973 a national conference wished there existed in society and in the Church "welcoming free spaces". Even if the experience catechumens have is

1. "This last standpoint is important. For it makes the possibility of baptism depend not only on the faith of the parents but also on the situation of the church into which the candidate may be baptised".

limited quantitatively, it has qualitatively the value of a sign. It becomes
plain that initiation to the christian faith is not only a matter for children,
and that on the other hand this initiation is ordinarily made according to
progressive stages, marked out with celebrations at intervals. Around the
year 1975, work for adult catechesis contributed also to manifesting the
importance of a faith-memory adequately and regularly rediscovered,
and sometimes even reinitiated in depth. Are not some adults, baptised
and therefore christian, sometimes just like catechumens? a long way
from the Gospel and christian experience, yet sometimes approachable
and sometimes even asking for an initiation suitable to their situation.

Around the same time on the other hand, infant catechesis started
imposing similar problems. It could not be done 'as if' all the children
to be catechised were practising. In many school chaplaincies it was
found necessary with children like this to follow a course which progressively developed their spiritual potential. It was in a way going back to
before their baptism so as to eventually rediscover with them one day
their baptismal faith. This was the 'chaplaincy catechesis' development.

Was it opportune, given this state of things, to reopen the issue of
general infant baptism? Some thought so: is it normal to appeal to
ecclesial faith following classical augustinian theology when the parents
have apparently no real attachment to this faith of the Church? Inversely, another development, pastoral and theological, arising from
'popular catholicism', underlines the fact that many people are not in a
position to confess the faith with the exactness clerically required. They
are no less a part of the Church, however. An ongoing debate which,
starting from catechesis, joins up with the continuing problem about
infant baptism.

Childhood catechesis

What children's catechesis contributes today to the study of initiation
is probably to be found less in this debate which is becoming heated and
polarised, and more, in the long term, in investment in what might
well be promising.

I should like in this connection to cite, from the nineteen-sixties and
until 1975, the theological study aroused on *confirmation*. This work
has, for the present, slowed down. No doubt to await the conclusion of
pastoral experimentation. But what it has already contributed has at
least allowed a rediscovery of the value of a sacrament which many a
short while ago were holding to be compromised and without much of
a future.

In the same way it appears to me that pastoral work with children,
after attempting to delineate what there might be of ambiguity in the
popular ceremony of solemn communion, is coming to rediscover the

sense of initiation to be found in the eucharist. This sacrament then takes on a hitherto unexpected significance and gives rise to preparation allowing the baptismal remembrance to be restored. As for solemn communion, inherited from the 17th century, it is replaced by festivals of faith which moreover maintain here and there the social features and standing which it had. As for the 'renovation', that has practically disappeared in favour of the festivals of faith. Not that these latter have in fact any actual reference to baptism. No doubt it is hardly possible to reactivate the baptismal remembrance on these occasions: the faith confessed at that age is formulated with the words and experiences of the moment and is not in a position to take on the baptismal sense. That will have to be done later, given another opportunity.

All the same, the pastoral ministry to children is remarkably on the way to rediscovering baptism by reason of the requests for the sacrament from *children of school age.* Such requests are quantitatively a notable factor in France today. In 1972 there was, besides, officially published a 'Rite for the baptism of children of catechetical age' (French version: 1977). It offers an initiation to the faith by stages, with a catechumenate slant. A first sign of a children's catechumenate, the possibility of which however frightens many when it is envisaged for newborn children.

Baptism immediately or deferred

In practice infant baptism remains today effectively the general custom. Two attempts at pastoral renewal are developing in this regard. The one seemingly bearing the most fruit is a preparation for baptism in which christians increasingly work with the priest and sometimes take over from him. We might just wish that there could be regularly offered to parents asking for baptism for their child and who are far from the faith, concrete possibilities of a catechumenate process adapted to their situation. The other attempt undertaken consists of suggesting to parents wishing to have their child baptised two possibilities for them to choose between after thinking it over: baptism immediately or later on. But where the choice in question is offered to parents, very few opt for a delayed baptism. This fact gives pause for thought.

Besides, this is understandable, given the vagueness of the future possibilities thus opened to them, whether from the standpoint of the parents, feeling uncertain about the time to come, or from that of the institutional Church, which has not always the means for accompanying parents and children in their discovery of the faith. Let me add that to present the parents with a choice is not self-evident in many cases. The more so, as social pressure in favour of immediate baptism is strong. The more so also, as the more well-informed sense the reservations of religious authorities at baptism being delayed.

F

What will come of it? It is useless to play the prophet. But for the moment it appears to me that 'deferred baptism' as a pastoral alternative has not had its last word. It is certainly not a matter of indiscretely imposing a delay in baptism on parents who would feel obliged to submit to a new authoritarianism. It is rather a matter of putting the problem of baptism in a broad perspective. In other words, the problem of faith and of initiation to the faith in our day. The suggestion of deferred baptism is only a means, not always suitable, of manifesting the seriousness of the questions thus raised.

Now this 'Operation — Truth', whatever its exact form, is a demanding one for those with pastoral responsibility. It faces them in effect with the realisation of their own baptism: how could they make others understand and want what baptism is and especially what it stands for, if they themselves do not live their own baptism?

There appears besides this a necessity for a pastoral ministry to the 'public at large' which would not be uniquely centred on practising catholics or militants and would know how to present the faith and what it calls for, in a way adapted to people far from the language and outlook of the 'conscious' Church (or said to be such).

There is finally the need to clarify what is meant by deferred baptism. If what is intended is a catechumenate course for parents as for the children, let this be said and the measures taken. It is not always possible, at least as things are. In any case the 'welcoming' or 'presentation', instead of being considered alternative ceremonies, oddities more or less, should appear plainly as a first stage in the initiation process, the beginning of baptism, its first act.

How not to replace
one ambiguity with another?

On the level of the universal Church these ideas are not necessarily the most apt for very varying situations. Besides, they appear surprising to authorities in Rome if we are to judge by the 'Instruction on infant baptism' published by the Congregation for Doctrine and the Faith in October 1980 and addressed to the bishops.

This text begins by noting the variations and uncertainties in the present situation. It recalls therefore the traditional and legitimate character of infant bapism and emphasises that the sacrament is not merely a sign but an efficacious cause with regard to the faith, and a witness to the divine initiative. That being said, it remains possible to 'defer' baptism, even to refuse it.[1] But the document multiplies recommendations to prudence in the matter. It expresses reservation notably

1. "Where these guarantees are not serious the decision can be made to defer the sacrament, even to refuse it if they are certainly void" (no. 28).

against a 'rite' of enrolment with a view to future baptism. And it explicitly adopts a stand against a rite of entry into the catechumenate.[1]

It is on these practical points that the document can cause difficulty. It is clear enough what is the intention of its authors. But it is not certain that these indications are all justified.

It is a matter, the text says expressly, of not giving to the wider, less informed, public the impression that the rite celebrated at birth is equivalent to baptism, when it is merely a gesture in the direction of the rite of baptism to be received later on. This is the important thing indeed. But yet it is the danger run perhaps by the new ritual for baptism of children of school age. This distinguishes stages of catechumenal type. And it even takes care to draw up a ceremony for inscribing the request for baptism before entry into the catechumenate proper. Certainly these two situations are not the same. We might indeed consider that in the baptism of a schoolchild, the ceremony of baptism proper is plainly on the horizon as a celebration for which preparation is undertaken and which will occur within a few months. The hesitation is much greater when it is a child just born who is welcomed and presented to God and the Church. Yet I wonder whether this difference entails a change of nature between the two situations. To my mind ambiguity is unavoidable in both cases. It is a part of any progression by stages: when the course is begun it is never absolutely certain that it will be completed.

I add that the ambiguity in question is probably the greater in that the practice on which it bears is still not very widespread. Supposing that in the coming years a greater number of ceremonies of children's reception were to be celebrated in France, it could well be that the public would realise that here was a first rite leading on to others later. Besides, that is how people already look at things: after a baby's baptism it is an understood thing that the people attending will 'meet again', for example for the child's 'communion'.

No wonder-formula

Basically I believe that we should not hide from ourselves the difficulties of a pastoral ministry where the newly-born are no longer always, or not necessarily, baptised. But are not the difficulties to which this is trying to respond greater still? The risk of being mistaken on the exact sense of a rite performed for a child, is that more serious than to

1. "The suggested enrolment with a view to a future catechumenate should not be accompanied by a rite to this effect, which would easily be taken for the equivalent of the sacrament itself. It must be clear also that this enrolment is not an entry into the catechumenate and that infants so enrolled cannot be considered catechumens with all the prerogatives attaching to that status" (no. 31).

go through the act of baptism with no understanding?

In another connection there has been the proposal of attacking possible misconceptions or misunderstandings by excluding any ritual act presupposing a request for future baptism. But in the short term also it would be a sign for the parents of the religious sense, even the gospel sense indeed, of the birth. Does not the above suggestion fail to recognise the legitimate need of celebration which many people feel in presence of the newborn child they have brought into the world? If the Church does not wish to rest content with sanctifying no more than the great occasions in human experience it is surely indispensable that this ceremony should not only be a celebration of the birth but should be explicitly directed towards baptism. Under the pretext that this term of reference is sometimes equivocal, must we suppress a ceremony which gathers the family together around the newborn child?

Newborn: a catechumen?

The Roman document requires furthermore that the newly-born should not be considered catechumens, so as not to give them a status in effect implying a personal free choice. But again I wonder whether this stance is entirely consonant with baptismal practice as a whole. Why such a restriction, when no difficulty is found in calling babies persons and effectively considering them as such? Of course it will be said that the paradox in baptising babies lies precisely in that the newly-born are baptised without being able to be catechumens, with no catechumenate. And it will be said in addition that the term catechumen should not be used lightly for fear of being speedily devalued and becoming commonplace, which would cancel out the contribution of the catechumenate movement to the contemporary Church. But these two objections do not appear to me to be decisive. Given the paradoxical nature which infant baptism necessarily has. Given above all the present need of the pastoral ministry to recognise the child just born as in reality a member of the Church, or at least effectively linked to her. A Church which supposedly contained within it no babies and was content to put them on a 'waiting list', would that still be the Church of the Gospel and of baptism?

Equally, too, it is by taking account of public opinion that I would wish newborn children to have, in the cases where immediate baptism did not apply, not only a simple enrolment with a view to a future catechumenate as in the ritual for children of school age, but a veritable entry into the catechumenate, that is to say into the Church. That allows of saying that the ceremony of welcoming the newborn child really is the beginning of baptism. And that upholds the tradition of a Church not afraid of including babies.

Entry into the Church before being baptised

For these reasons it appears to me therefore that the welcoming or presentation of a baby should take on a stronger meaning than mere enrolment. This implies certain risks: that of a possible confusion of this ceremony with baptism proper; that of starting a process which will not necessarily be continued later. Two 'normal' risks and probably unavoidable. Wanting to pass immediately to the pastoral position — theoretically the most clear — enrolment with a view to future catechumenate minimises both the paradox produced today as yesterday for society or for the Church by the newborn child, and popular difficulties over accepting a ceremony not yet an integrating part of baptismal ritual.

This standpoint brings in a somewhat unexpected theological problem. It is this: is it possible to dissociate in time the effects commonly recognised of baptism and in practice to enter the Church before entering fully into baptism? In fact this type of question has long ago received its answer in the practice of a catechumenate. With adult candidates for baptism it is so. That means that baptism by stages has ecclesial effects which are manifested even before personal profession of faith is possible and baptism can take place. Therefore it is possible to say that a person enters the Church because of a baptism to come but also in order to be able to find in it the meaning of the act of baptism. It is baptism which gives entry into the Church. But it is the Church which makes us enter into baptism.

*   *   *

Statement of accounts

Sum total: what in the 20th century should we retain from the history of christian initiation in the West?

— It certainly appears that in our day we tend to situate every individual question in a *context* which enlarges its scope. So it is that the question under debate is less one of baptism, *a fortiori* infant baptism, than one of initiation into the Gospel and the christian faith.

— It is equally plain that christian initiation has its probably irreducible share of *ambivalence*. This appears clearly in regard to infant baptism. Theology enunciates its effects as indicated in Scripture and as understood by church tradition. But equally, public opinion on its side imputes to this same baptism effects which are not altogether conformable to those enunciated by theology. In particular, to have children christened can simply mean the wish to carry on a family or social tradition. This is better than nothing, as we have come to see in these last few years. But it is not everything. And it is not so easy to say exactly what is the existing relationship between this social tradition and the church allegiance treated of in theology.

— In any case it seems that *initiation into the faith* is becoming pluralistic. Which is normal in a society like ours. Baptism in particular is taking on several aspects: adult catechumens, children of school age, the newly-born. Is this diversity harmful to ecclesial unity? Or does it rather express the unlimited extent of the one gospel faith? Here there is a problem at once theoretical and practical which only experience can decide.

— But this diversity leads on to an experiment arousing interest, a stimulating rediscovery: I am speaking of the *progression by stages* normally undertaken by christian initiation. It had been forgotten. Or at least until now children's catechesis and that of adults were not always linked up with the sacramental rites of initiation. Now we are beginning to do this much more.

— It remains that in the Church as a whole christian *consciousness* of initiation is still limited. Pastoral work is doubtless suffering from the deficiency.

8

To be christian
is to be received into the Church

It starts with a request

How does christian initiation begin?

I should like to answer this question by considering three rites of baptism at present in use in the Latin Church and by referring also as the case requires to the Orthodox and Reformed Churches.[1]

In addition, my emphasis is that the beginning of initiation does not coincide precisely with the beginning of faith or of conversion. This appears fairly clearly in the case of adult candidates for baptism. They have been, most often, faced with the Gospel and called to the faith, some time before taking any steps leading them in the direction of the Church and the sacraments of initiation. And fundamentally it is always God who takes the first step and awakens in the heart of a human being the desire of being christian. But initiation as such starts when a request is made of the Church. And for the newly-born it begins when the parents expressly desire their children to be baptised or, less often, received by the Church while waiting until they themselves can ask for baptism.

Consequently initiation starts long before the outset of the celebration proper of any church rite. It starts when a request is made and finds an answering echo in the Church. Which implies a meeting between one not initiated and one or more christians, dialogue, discovery of the Gospel, and even a certain catechesis.

The fact that christian initiation is set in motion by a request appears to me of capital importance. Not only to indicate the free-will in the process, that of the future baptised themselves or that of the parents presenting their child. But especially for the initiation to be borne along by a desire and an expectation, in other words by the dynamism of 'mystagogia'.

Therefore it is not surprising that this request should be emphasised at the time of the first liturgical celebration in which welcoming into

1. For the Churches of the Reform, see J. J. von Allmen, *Pastorale du baptême*, Cerf, 1978. For the Churches of the East. I-H. Dalmais, *Liturgies d'Orient*, Cerf, 1980.

the Church is expressed. In the present ritual for infant baptism, reference is made to it at the very beginning of the baptismal liturgy: "What do you ask of God's Church for N.?" The formula is practically the same for the ceremony of reception of adult catechumens. The ritual for the baptising of children of school age goes further.[1] It emphasises the request, to the point of celebrating it as such as soon as the child expresses it,[2] before going on to the welcome proper on the Church's part,[3] which will give rise to another celebration. In certain cases for adults the same way of doing things, not provided officially, could be useful. It would allow taking into account the search which has been undertaken without waiting for it to be sufficiently advanced to end in an explicit, official, reception into the Church.

Without going into these details, the ritual for infant baptism is not any the more behindhand in emphasising the importance of the request. It reintroduces it just before the pouring of the water: "Is it your will that N. should be baptised in the faith of the Church, which we have all professed with you?" This repetition does not appear in the rite of baptism for children of school age, doubtless because it has been especially made clear at the start, doubtless also because the child is big enough to express by being there and participating, the intention already formulated in what went before.[4]

What is requested?

Christian initiation begins therefore with a request. And the liturgy makes much of this essential point of departure.

But what exactly is requested?

There are formulas ready to hand, suggested by the rituals or in booklets of preparation for baptism. But there is above all what the people themselves express and which does not necessarily correspond, especially at the outset, to what the liturgy proposes. And it is desirable that the request should be thus expressed in the spontaneous form given it by adults presenting themselves to the Church on their own account or for their newborn child.

1. Rite of Initiation for Children of Catechetical Age (French adaptation, 1977).
2. This preliminary stage is called 'Reception by the Church of the request for baptism'.
3. This reception keeps its ancient name, a little constrained, of 'entry into the catechumenate'.
4. For adults there is indeed in the present ritual a reformulation of the initial request in a ceremony at the beginning of Lent when the catechumens are 'called' to the sacraments of the faith. I shall come back to this. I merely add here that this repetition of the initial request is not provided in the rite leading to confirmation and first communion. This is significant: baptism received suffices as an introduction to these sacraments.

What is requested? That can vary a good deal. A desire to be like the others who are christians; for parents, to continue the family christening tradition. Equally a person might want to become a christian, which can be expressed in a variety of ways. Lastly a person might decide on the sacraments themselves: "I want to be baptised".[1] It can be understood therefore that the request needs to be particularised. And this is what is aimed at by the stages of the catechumenate course, or conversations and interchanges in a preparation of parents for the baptism of their child.

How does this 'decanting' work? From the 3rd century the 'Apostolic Tradition' of Hippolytus sets out in some detail a process of discernment. There is a first examen, that of the newcomers. They are asked "for what reason they are seeking the faith". It is verified from the people accompanying them "whether they are capable of listening". Finally their "manner of living" is examined. That is, what might in practice favour or on the contrary impede christian living eventually: are they celibate or married? free in act and deed or under the yoke of slavery? The text of Hippolytus above all pays great attention to the occupations exercised by the candidates for christianity: some are contrary to the Gospel, for example those which are immoral or which oblige to pagan religious practices. Then, several years later, when the catechesis has run its course, a second examen takes place with the aim of verifying whether the postulants have been leading a life in accordance with their beliefs. Thus those who are to receive baptism are 'chosen' people, 'elect'.

Certainly times have changed. But is the principle of such a discernment out of date? To be a christian is not compatible with any and every kind of actual way of life. It is not to be reduced to a private adherence to a few beliefs divorced from the choices of day-to-day living.

What is equally striking in the 3rd century method — Tertullian at about the same period gives a like witness — is that the initial request made by those presenting themselves to the Church is being 'taken in charge' by the Church in a kind of interchange between those asking and those of whom the request is made. There is also room in this relationship for third parties, those accompanying the candidate and who will become godfather and godmother. In short, the request for baptism formulated in personal fashion at the outset becomes more and more a matter for the Church. In the end what is being asked is what

1. This 'popular' formula reduces the sacraments of initiation to baptism alone and, besides, reduces initiation to the single fact of baptism. Obviously this is insufficient. But as a starting point it is very significant: it shows that faith and belonging to the Church can be confirmed by an objective act.

the person has learned to ask. The initial intention is reworked by progressive experience.

In the present Roman ritual the formulas do also express this situation. The priest puts a question: What is it you ask? In the original
sense of the words he puts 'in question' the request made earlier. Then
he reformulates the reply which he has received and asks the adult candidate or the baby's parents for their agreement to the new formula.[1]
Clerical bombast? Perhaps. But also evidence of what initiation is:
neophytes do not make their own definition of what is required.[2]

Request and promise

We may wonder whether the request for initiation, recast or intensi-
fied by the Church, does in effect result in a promise or engagement.
This point is often raised concerning infant baptism. And it is easy to
see why. If there is a promise right at the beginning of initiation, can
adults promise in the name of the child and commit themselves in place
of the child?

In fact, in the early Church the word 'promise' appears regularly in
the texts relating to baptism. Thus Justin: "Those who believe in the
truth of our teaching and our doctrine promise to live according to this
law".[3] In the 3rd century the term is met in Tertullian. And already the
question put today about baptism of the newly-born is plainly addressed:
"It is better to defer baptism, especially in the case of very young
children. For why, if there is no pressing necessity, expose those presenting the child to a very grave peril? They could die without being
able to fulfil their promises. If they live, the children may turn out
badly and deceive their hopes".[4] On the other hand Tertullian introduces into christian language the word *sacramentum* which has at once
the sense of engagement and of oath. The two problems raised by the
concept of baptismal promises, and which need to be carefully distinguished, are thus characterised: can we promise in place of the children? and besides, what is the meaning in any case of baptism understood as a promise?

The first question is in the end a simple one. At the baptism of a
newborn child the adults certainly engage to give the child the opportunities and means of believing, knowing what it is that they are about.

1. There is an alternative formula in the reception of adults: "Do you agree
to all these things?" For reception of infants or school-age children in the
French edition the priest counters with a practical question: "Are you prepared
to do this?" "Do you want to join us?"
2. Dialogue is in the most exact sense a part of initiation and of christian
sacramentality.
3. First Apologia, no. 61.
4. De Baptismo, no. 18.

In this sense they certainly undertake a commitment. But it is a commitment which concerns themselves, not a commitment in the child's place. The early rituals were fairly ambiguous on this point. And it was in fact for this reason that the Reformed ritual of Zwingli reformulated the 'vows' in the baptism ceremony.[1] The Catholic ritual of 1614 kept the traditional formulas as they were: the godfather and godmother made as though speaking in the name of the child. But the 1969 ritual removes all misunderstanding: the parents, godfather and godmother speak in their own name as adults. And besides it is not a promise exactly that is asked of them; it is enough for them to know what they will have to do.[2]

That being said, we might wonder whether the expression 'baptismal promises' is altogether advisable. It is certainly, let me repeat, not rare in the early Church.[3] And it well expresses the serious commitment to the confession of faith along with the renunciation of evil and the spirit of evil. Moreover, now when christian life is seeking to become again more conscious of baptism it is not surprising that it should look for the sense of that covenant which baptism imparts to our life.[4] But it is a characteristic of the recent official texts that they hardly ever use this expression.

When God commits himself
man can commit himself

Why that reservation? Is it out of an ambiguous adaptation to modern sensibilities, which no longer dare commitment? I think rather that the question raised today in intellectual circles as a result of a great sense of a child's autonomy will lead to a reappraisal of the deeper implications of christian initiation. It is not in the first place a human promise which is made at baptism but a profession of faith. If there is a promise

1. 'Reflexions of a protestant on general infant baptism', article by Pastor von Allmen. The author regrets this alteration (he even speaks of a 'suppression'), which leads to no longer underlining the parents' commitment to bring up their child in the faith. It seems to him to devalue the expression of faith in the baptism ceremony. See also, by the same author, *Pastorale du baptême*, Cerf, 1978.

2. "Do you clearly understand what you are undertaking?" is asked of the parents. "Are you ready to help the parents of this child in their duty as christian parents?" is asked of the godparents.

3. For example: Theodore of Mopsuestia ("you must promise to turn away from the devil", Catechetical homily 21, 13,5). Gregory of Nazianzen ("what danger do we not run by transgressing engagements made to God?", Sermon no. 40,8) John Chrysostom ("you who are going to be baptised, learn I beg you the formula of your covenant with the Lord", Second Catechesis, no. 4).

4. The expression 'baptismal promises' was popularised in France in the 17th and 18th centuries with the rise of the parish missions. But the phrase is already to be found in the catechism of the Council of Trent.

at a baptism it is God's.[1] If there is a commitment in christian initiation, it is God's first of all.

Of course this commitment by God reaches — and liberates — all the baptised whatever their age. Therefore there is indeed a human commitment in christian initiation. It is that implied by the request, and authorised by the action of God. But this commitment is both more and less than a promise. More than a promise, for it is a decisive and vital relationship between a human being and the living God. Less than a promise, for such an engagement always contains a particle of risk, it is so comprehensive and final.

I do not say therefore that the baby is committed to a promise by the baptism just received, and still less that the parents engage the child. But those who have presented the child are committed by the process they have undertaken, the Church is committed by the ceremony she causes to be performed in her name, and God is committed by the gift he has given. All this is imparted to the child in a way we do not comprehend: henceforward the child has the potential to make a commitment when the time comes.[2] As for adults just baptised, they have effectively undertaken a commitment and this term is no doubt preferable to that of promise. But they have to live it and discover its full significance: this they will do throughout their lives by making remembrance of what was done for them. They are committed but they have yet to discover what this means for them.

Initiation and catechesis

If it takes time to get baptised it is because it takes time to enter into the mystery in reality and be able to 'stay' in it. The early christians made much of the 'catechesis'[3] from this point of view, that is to say a handing on of the mysteries of the faith with their spiritual and practical savour and their inter-relationship. Catechetical work today will gain by referring back to the understanding of the early Church when, without previous experience, people had to face up to the demands and requirements of the Gospel.

1. Strictly speaking the child is put into the position to make a commitment, is inscribed in a historical tradition and a nearness to God which, in theory, can bring the child to take on itself what has been done for it.
2. The rite of adult baptism does not use the word 'promise' except when speaking of the divine promise. ("Bless our brothers and sisters as they earnestly prepare themelves for baptism. Be true to your promise: make them holy in preparation for you". The Rites, p. 58, at the blessing of the catechumens.)
3. The word 'catechesis', now commonly used, has etymologically an exact bearing: it concerns making 'resound' (in the word 'catechesis', there is the word for 'echo') the Word of God, and that 'from above down' (cata, in greek), i.e. starting from God who reveals himself, down to the will and heart of the one who is opening to the faith.

In this sense I should like to note the importance ascribed to the 'desire' of discovering about the faith. It is especially Augustine who emphasises this disposition, indispensable in his view for anyone receiving the catechesis.[1] Without such an attitude nothing takes effect. There is therefore often an effort to be made to "lead a person to desire what through error or dissembling was not desired until then."[2]

On this point it must be clearly understood that the desire for God and the Gospel can never be *a priori* presupposed. Parents can ask for baptism for their child without claiming to be truly desirous of discovering the nature of the christian mystery. Similarly adults can ask the Church for information about what she believes, because they have been in contact with a christian or else because they feel a need to find out about christianity, without necessarily having, especially at the beginning, the intention of themselves becoming christians. In some cases such requests end by a real desire for the faith. Something is stirred in the one who before was merely interested. A mysterious attraction forms which from then on carries the process forward and gives it life. But for others nothing of the kind occurs. The Gospel awakens no overtones in them. They hear it as a message which is rather dull and tiresome, like an impossible utopia or again like a type of religious experience not corresponding to what they feel themselves.

A strange mystery, the action of faith. From God's side, no doubt. But also from the human side. Some, because of the circumstances of their life or their temperament, are 'sensitised' to the Gospel. Others remain cold and closed to it, without this attitude being necessarily a want of courage or seriousness on their part. Formerly, in a society more homogeneous, where christianity benefited from a kind of general consensus, there was hardly occasion or possibility for such want of response. Today, in a social context where the choice of believing is offered to each one, such cases are not unusual.

Transmitting the word and actions of faith

In the early Church, catechesis was one of the points to which most attention was given. It was not enough to proclaim the Gospel or invite people to come to Christ. It was also held necessary to allow those who desired it to become in reality and progressively bearers of the gospel attitudes and convictions. The christian communities took great care

1. De catechizandis rudibus, 5.9.
2 The Bishop of Hippo wrote a little guide to the catechism in response to a request from a deacon of Carthage who felt in difficulties over his role as catechist. It is the famous *De catechizandis rudibus* (=how to catechise beginners). Augustine emphasises what it means to 'want to become a christian' (5,9). In the Sermon 216 are the typical words: "Love what you will be" (no. 8).

over this deep and integrated evangelisation.

How was it done in practice?

What is striking when we look at the practices of the first centuries of christianity is that the catechesis co-ordinated various situations deemed favourable and complementary. In particular it articulated the relationship between two persons, the catechist and the newcomer to the faith, with wide-ranging meetings in the framework of a group of catechumens with the christians training them.

This way of doing things can be of interest in our age. It reminds us that the collective aspect does not in fact exclude a certain individuation. Catechesis should ideally connect the two. This applies doubtless for the children under catechesis. The catechetical classes should allow all to be themselves. But that is equally indispensable for adults. I am thinking of parents of children for whom they are asking baptism, of young people preparing for marriage. Some of them will never really speak in a group. They don't dare. Or else they do not really feel at ease for cultural reasons. How are they to be allowed to have their say and to 'react' in their own way? Isn't it useful sometimes for christians to meet at home for a more private exchange? I have in mind likewise adults desirous of beginning to believe again, 'starting again from scratch'. I have often noticed that in such cases, gatherings are not enough. They must be accompanied by more personal dialogue. For Justin, Hippolytus or Augustine the 'personalised' phase of the catechesis was a church ceremony which normally began christian initiation.

Another characteristic of catechesis equally emphasised in the early Church: in the first centuries of christianity it was plain that catechesis was not over when the sacramental rites had been celebrated. It called normally for a continuation, precisely so as to go back, after the main rites of water, oil, and communion, over what had been given in the celebration. They talked it over. And this was the point in the catechesis called 'mystagogical', i.e. according to the greek meaning of the term capable of leading to the mysteries. This custom was not only pedagogical. It had a theological sense. The mystagogical catechesis went from the liturgical or sacramental mysteries to the mysteries of faith made present by the rites, entering into human time but always before and beyond what we can grasp.

This concept certainly is not earlier than the 4th century. It is besides, perhaps, more eastern than western. Doubtless also it is bound up with the desire not to divulge to all and sundry what was the heart of the mystery.[1] But it is at the same time quite characteristic of the trans-

---

1. "If after catechesis a beginner in the catechumenate asks what has been said, do not give anything away to this person outside . . . a catechumen who

mission of the words and actions of the faith. The symbols must speak for themselves, they risk losing their force by being watered down in interminable commentaries and a flow of explanations. Let them be allowed their unexpectedness and then they speak, they inspire speech. Catechesis has prepared for them. But in their turn they prepare for a new form of catechesis which will spring from them.

Let me add that remembering the early Church reminds us of an obvious fact sometimes misunderstood today. The transmission of the faith is not reduced to a communication of beliefs or, according to the modern way, a debate and a confrontation of ideas. It follows a series of rites, that is to say symbolic gestures. Hence the 'stages' which traditionally constitute adult baptism and which baptism for children of school age has just discovered. They signify that the discovery of the faith needs to be expressed in prayer and in ritual, long before the rite of water. Contemporary christianity is finding itself faced here with a great deal to be considered. Certainly it is not lacking in a taste for celebration. And we cannot fail to rejoice that on the whole baptisms, confirmations, and first communions, are celebrated with care, joy and simplicity. But we lack the form of celebration suited to the manner of believing of many people who do not feel 'at home' yet in the eucharist and yet who would like rather more than the occasional meeting. We need celebrations allowing people already baptised but still at the opening stages of faith, to experience, if they so wish, physically and as time goes on, the concrete significance of the Gospel. It is not enough for this to apply the faith of the Gospel to the things of everyday life.

Recitation and Credo

I should like once more to point out how the content of the catechesis can be organised in various ways according to the understanding of the early Church. Catechesis of course always aims at leading on to mystery and to reveal the essence of what is communicated. But while this latter aim is always the same and care for a certain coherence remains constant, 'plans' or 'courses' can vary. Which, it appears to me, connects up with highly contemporary debate. The catechists of today who ask for a standard syllabus should be reminded that the best road to take is the

hears something from one of the faithful gets upset as he does not understand what he hears, criticises the matter and mocks at what is said to him. For you are on the threshold. Watch therefore that you do not speak. Not that what is said to you is not worthy of being repeated. But there are ears you might confide in which are not ready to receive it. When from experience you know the sublimity of what we are teaching you, then you will understand that you must keep silence" (Cyril of Jerusalem, Sixth Catechesis, 'To those who are to be illumined', 19,12). Notice the expression 'from experience'. We have met this already.

one adapted to the person or group they are preparing and therefore they have to be continually adapting. That does not prevent the existence of certain general guide-lines. But it cuts out strict uniform programming.

In Antiquity, three principles for catechesis seem to have counted especially.

First of all, what is sometimes called the catechesis of the 'two ways'. In the 2nd century, the Didache (= teaching of the apostles), which has kept for us some very ancient baptismal references, presents two ways in opposition, the way of life and the way of death. It is a theme of jewish origin which the Gospel is itself echoing (Mt 7, 13–14). We might think that this manner of presenting christianity, which must besides suit the beginnings of catechesis, risks being moralising or artificially accentuating the dramatic in faith and salvation. And yet this type of catechesis, popular in style, has the advantage of presenting a choice to be made. It tends to call for a decision, and does not have the newcomer complacent over religious knowledge or information that has been acquired.

This ancient scheme was complemented significantly in the early Church by two other models. First there was that of Augustine called *recitation*, that is to say the recital of the history of revelation and of salvation. A mark of christianity not in the first place a system but a collection of happenings of which remembrance can be made. Next, that called the *Credo*, the symbol of faith. From the 2nd century, with the '*Demonstration of apostolic preaching*' of Irenaeus, then with the baptismal creeds of the 3rd century, the importance taken by this synthesis of christian beliefs is clear to see. The Latin Church kept a Roman baptismal symbol which we call 'The Apostles' Creed'. But this is a detailed symbol, honed by the Councils and weighted with theological exactitudes, used by the Latin Church in the eucharist. And the difference between these two formularies is characteristic: the faith celebrated in the eucharist, that is, the weekly celebration in the Church's life, needs to be precise in regard to the basic faith into which christians are baptised.

Recitation and *Credo*: two ways, fundamentally, of stating the faith. The first is basic. It corresponds to the preaching of the Gospel. The second serves as norm or reference. However, it keeps behind its doctrinal form the style of the gospel narrative. It has the value of a synthesis. It is in this ancient confession of faith which spread throughout practically all the Churches that a person is baptised.[1] And it is this we are invited to commit to memory.[2]

1. Before the rite of water, the Roman ritual provides, at least since the 3rd century, 'questions on the faith'. These are modelled on the three articles of

Course of catechesis

How do things stand today with catechetical courses? It is already significant that we speak of courses rather than programmes. More especially in France the appearance of a selection called *'Pierres vivantes'* has aroused a series of quite varied suggestions. Starting from the one collection of passages, meditations, and pictures, several directions are possible. The structure of children's catechesis in successive years and an organised progression offers common meeting points in these various itineraries.

For adults, the experience of the catechumenate arrives at similar conclusions. A really catechumen-centred catechesis does not aim at deepening or recentring an experience and knowledge of the faith thought to be more or less already acquired. It intends to be foundational and forward-moving. Without following strict rules it ordinarily takes various stages which can be schematised as follows.

At first stage, after the request has been made, consists in clarifying expectations and implications. Often it is here a matter of dialogue 'turn about', starting with questions raised by the person desirous of finding out what it means to believe.

Then gradually and the most often at the time of entering the Church a more organised catechesis is built up, centred on the Gospel and the Old Testament, in other words the biblical revelation.

Finally, as the essential rites of initiation approach it becomes indispensable to speak of the sacraments of the Church, its mission in the

the Creed. The eastern rites keep to the recital of the Credo proper (that of Nicaea, except in the coptic and chaldaic rites). This was equally the case in the Roman liturgy until 1969: the godparents knew they would have to 'say the Creed'. This use which often doubled with the profession of faith in question and answer form, has been suppressed. But the Creed has not for all that been dropped from the baptism ceremony (I have heard regrets over its disappearance!). The recital of the Creed goes back to a rite appearing in the 4th century attested by Augustine in the 5th century. Just before the baptism itself, the Creed was 'handed over' ('tradition') to the catechumens who had to say it ('rendition') a week later.

2. In the 4th century, the Creed was given orally to those who were to be illumined. There was no question of writing it. Augustine insists on this. And today when we are trying to recover the remembrance of baptism, it is interesting to note this part played by the memory in the preparation for the baptismal rite: "In order to retain this symbol word for word, you should not write it, but learn it by hearing it" (Sermon, 212). "Let no one be anxious and let not anxiety hold anyone back. Have confidence . . . If anyone makes a mistake in the words let him at least make no mistake about the faith" (G. Morin, 1.1).

world and its Credo.[1] This third stage consists in practice of building on
what has been already assimilated by going on into practical and concrete discovering of the mystery of faith. One can speak of the sacraments and particularly of baptism and the eucharist, even of confirmation,[2] because experience has been gained of celebrating the faith and the
gifts of God in the rites already attended. There can be a deepening of
the sense of the Church, its structure and its aspirations, its goal and its
difficulties, because there is already a certain experience of ecclesial
solidarity. Finally can come the profession of faith, intended less to fix
in the mind the spiritual discovery made in one of the canonical texts,
than to return to what has already been received, check for its essential
consistency and possible gaps. You can see that this third stage of the
catechesis, therefore, consists in passing from the biblical and evangelical to the Church's Credo.

Entering the Church

Let us take the case of school children or adults advancing in the
discovery and apprenticeship of the faith. We will suppose therefore
that the original request has been deepened, time has been taken for it
to mature, and the catechesis has done its work. The moment comes
when what has been accomplished must be signified, officially noted,
celebrated before God and the Church.

From the point of view of a child's development or that of a catechumen, that moment can be pinpointed. He or she who is opening to the
Word of God and to the christian experience feels the need to be received into the Church which is gradually characterising their life. They
are in a position to express something of their growing faith.

From the catechetical point of view this characteristic moment corresponds — especially for adult catechumens — to the beginning or the
middle of the second period that I have just been indicating. A first
comprehensive review has been made and now they are entering on a
more organised, more exact, discovery of Scripture.

The moment of transition determined in this way is celebrated in the
Latin liturgy by a liturgical act called 'reception': the ecclesial community receives a person or persons who present themselves to it and

1. A team for the catechumenate at Lyons has published a popular christian
presentation in catechumenal style under the pseudonym of Thomas Pascal
and with the overall title *Découvrir le christianisme* (Fayard-Mame). The
four books give the possibility of drawing up an individual or group course:
Believing, let's speak about it (Bk 1), Believing, how do they do it? (Bk 2),
Believing in Him (Bk 3), Believing in practice (Bk 4).
2. This nuance regarding confirmation does not indicate any reservations
concerning it but takes account of the practice as it stands. Whether for
children of school age or for adults on their way to baptism, confirmation is
as a fact seen as following on admittance to the sacrament of the eucharist.

are going to take their place in it. Other expressions are possible to refer to this celebration: for example 'presentation' or again 'entry into the Church'.[1] The terminology is not very fixed. But whatever the words used, whichever phrase is thought best adapted to the sensitivities of the interested persons, it is certainly a reception which is being considered. With the twofold aspect implied by any reception: there are those welcoming and those welcomed. With, also, the conviction traditional in the Church according to which the rite of reception precedes the rite of baptism. The Church could not wash in the water of baptism someone she had not first fraternally and cordially received among her members.

Whether it is a question of newborn children, children at school, or adults, this celebration has therefore a fundamental meaning.

A welcoming Church

If we are seeking to give an explanation of this it appears a good thing to me to emphasise first of all that it is one or more persons entering the Church. They are not yet baptised, but they are already recognised as members of the Church. This is a sign of renewal for the christians baptised some time ago: newcomers are joining them.[2] It is equally the mark of a mysterious solidarity between different people drawn by a same Gospel.[3]

On the other hand the Church which will baptise begins by being the Church which welcomes. This welcome requires preparation on both sides. By the christians and the ministers of the celebration so that they can know these newcomers and their culture, can tell their background and their way of believing. And by the people being welcomed, as what is being offered them requires a renunciation without which there is no real entrance into the gospel mystery. It is desirable from this point of view that parents and godparents should themselves have followed some part of the road taken by the school children and adults received with a view to baptism. Basically the parents and godparents are welcomed

1. The word 'presentation' is often employed by evangelical christians. The word 'entry' is used in the Roman Catholic ritual to mean the welcoming of adults into the Church. The rite speaks in fact of 'admission to the catechumenate'. Perhaps it would be better to speak more fundamentally of 'admission into the Church': for this is what is meant, the catechumenate being the form of church membership for non-baptised persons who are intending baptism.

2. The president at the celebration (priest, minister, deacon) does not suffice on his own to represent the whole ecclesial assembly.

3. The catechumens, received liturgically but not yet baptised, are already part of the Church. It is to be regretted that the new juridical Code of Canon Law in the Latin Church does not bring this out: cf. Vatican II, *Lumen Gentium*, no. 14.

by the Church, by the ecclesial community, so that they can be true welcomers for these newborn children for whom they have just taken responsibility.

I would add that this reception, sometimes ambivalent considering the want of faith of some parents, is a joyous welcome. Not only because this is fitting or courteous. But more profoundly because the Church could not receive anyone except in good heart. Certainly she expects those who want to become her members or who want to present a newborn child, to have a minimum comprehension of what she lives by. But this reception, if it is 'oriented' to the future and the baptismal life, is not calculated. It includes therefore a possibility of being without any real outcome. I do not say this to discourage indispensable efforts at preparation for the celebration. But I note it here because it is part of the risk the Church takes on, the more freely that she is working elsewhere to rectify the situation created by requests for baptism which are all too unenligthened. The christian community, without naive sentimentality but also without morbid scrupulosity, gladly welcomes the newly-born. The Church truly receives them among the numbers of her members. But she feels herself bound to do all she can so that the adults presenting them can truly find or rediscover what their position is in her.

In any event, and this is the final aspect of the entry of newcomers into the Church, all present are called together to accept the word and the gift of God. They receive each other in receiving the Gospel. They express to one another the goodwill of God to all people. Receiving and received celebrate the reception which God makes of both in his Church and in the world in which he has placed them.

Receiving a name

Entry or reception into the Church is performed liturgically by means of three elements: a verbal exchange between the people present, a rite performed over those later to be baptised, a period of reading the Word of God and prayer. Other factors also enter into account, of course: preparation for the celebration, the setting in which it takes place, perhaps music and flowers.

The present catholic ritual adapts the celebration according to the situation of those being received: infants newborn, older children, adults. But the three main elements I have just mentioned are found in each.

The initial verbal exchange is set out in full. There is a greeting, people say why they are there and what they are going to do. A newcomer old enough for it obviously takes part in this dialogue, with its bearing on that person's request and decision.

All the same, in the ceremony of infant baptism there is one quite remarkable feature: "What name have you given the child?" Which is to say in fact: which christian name? And everyone knows this name already. So why ask the question? It may be it expresses a care to personalise the welcome into the Church: the newborn child is not an anonymous number. And in fact in the rites of reception provided for older children and for adults, mention of their christian name is made quite naturally. But in these two cases this mention is not underlined as in the case of babies. Is it insisted on in the initiation of newborn children as a reminder of the choice recently made in naming the child? This is not impossible.[1] But as a fact, the question concerning the christian name transposes an ancient rite still in use for adult initiation, known as 'the election'. After being received into the Church, after some time of church life, adults asking to be baptised are officially called, by their name, to take part in the sacrament of initiation. This ceremony has not remained in the rite for infants and I shall show the reason. Neither has it been retained by the editors of the initiation ritual for school-age children and I shall equally say why. But there is this trace left in the ritual for the newly-born.

It is only a trace. And at the same time it is a quite noteworthy modification of the old rite of final calling. The newborn who are received into the Church are not all called to go on to baptism: that would no doubt be superfluous seeing that the baptism is about to be celebrated in a few moments. But they are named. And that in a way intended to be official, which relates it to the same purpose in the election. God who gives his own Name to humans, reveals himself to them, is also he who calls us by our name.

The sign of reception

The action which signifies reception into the Church is the sign of the cross: "I claim you for Christ our saviour by the sign of his cross".[2] The parents and godparents make the same action. This therefore is the signing with the cross on the body of one whom Christ receives into his ecclesial body.

1. In the byzantine, syrian and maronite ordines there is a prayer 'for the giving of the name'. This prayer is said in the family, eight days following the birth, and no longer forms part of the baptismal liturgy as such. But this custom, similar to the one practised in judaism at the time of circumcision, gives weight to a feature which could well be not without importance for parents. We might wonder indeed whether, in certain cases, the rite of naming as it is given in the Roman ritual for infants could not bring in a blessing of the child by the parents. In other words, could not the byzantine and the latin practices be combined? Allowing that is, as I am about to say, that the rite of naming in the latin liturgy is not a rite for giving the name.

2. For adults, the sign of the cross can be given on the various senses. And it calls forth the response: Amen.

In liturgical history other actions have been used. For example, in Gaul in the 4th century there was a laying on of hands on those to be baptised which was a way of showing that the christian community had taken the new converts under their charge. Or again other gestures can be used in association with the sign of the cross. The Byzantines add to it the imposition of hands. With the Copts there is an anointing with oil which accompanies the marking with the cross. Quite often in the East a prayer and gesture of deliverance, which were not introduced into the western tradition until later, follow straight after the church reception. Until 1969 there was here in the Roman ritual a gesture unknown in the East, giving a little salt to the new members of the Church. This rite, certainly of popular origin, disappeared at the recent revision, no doubt because too much of a good thing.[1] But it is quite conceivable that other gestures of reception might be established in the future, as is already the case in some African churches.

Itinerary of the Word

Reception into the Church closes with a liturgy of the Word. The one who is received, if an adult, is already used to hearing this Word. And the parents presenting a child to the Church for the child to become a christian have perhaps some knowledge of the Word. In any case how could the Church's welcome be better expressed than to begin doing with the newcomer what is the great work of the Church, proclaiming and hearing the Word of God. The Church is a people gathered to hear his Word.

The baptismal rite for adults and that for school children both offer this liturgy of the Word. Before 1969 the ritual for infants had allowed this time of listening and welcome to disappear. Vatican II desires its return in accordance with the ancient western liturgy and the byzantine. The new ritual of 1969 carries it therefore.

I should like simply to underline this significant activity of the Word of God in the Church. The liturgy comprises in fact after the reading a homily and a prayer. Such is the movement of the Word in believers newly come to the Church or christians of longer date: they receive it, it is unfolded to them with today's words and today's preoccupations, and prolonged in a prayer of thanksgiving and fidelity.[2]

1. Symbol of preservation from corruption, or sign of the savour of a life with God.
2. The rituals suggest forms of prayer with 'intentions', like those in the Sunday Mass. Stress is laid therefore not only on those to be baptised but equally on the Church and on the world. The children's rite introduces at the end a new element not in the other Roman rituals: the invocation of the saints. Prayer amplified. Probably also an allusion to the Easter Vigil rite.

*   *   *

Summary

What shall we retain from these preliminary rites of christian initiation?

— Initiation begins with a request, continuing with it, becoming more defined, more evangelical, thereby expressing the spiritual longing of the person entering on christianity.

— Since the 3rd century, entry is made into the Church before entering baptism. That is, the Church gathers together human beings not all committed to Christ in the same way. The presence of catechumens and, in a different way, children under catechesis, or adults undergoing 're-initiation' shows therefore that initiation is a responsibility of the Church, operating within the christian group itself.

— Reception into the Church operates at the meeting-point of three desires, that of the person asking to be received, that of God building up his Church in the world, that finally of the Church whose care over discernment does not alter her joy at welcoming.

— It is quite meaningful to notice the forms taken on by the Church: she sees herself in the newcomers bringing a fresh breath of air and the exacting demands of beginners, she is symbolised in the liturgical minister presiding over the ceremonies and signifying God's commitment, she expresses herself through those called godparents who are at the same time on the side of the welcomed and the welcoming, she feels in solidarity with those taking part in the ceremonies without perhaps really participating in the mystery, she stands under the sign of the cross and the Word.

— Finally, we should keep the ceremony of reception as it was for centuries, an action on its own, before baptism. The sole practice of infant baptism, suppressing this separation and bringing together into one the ceremony of reception and that of baptism proper, ended by making it drop out of use. In our time the ceremony of reception, for adults, for children of school age, and also sometimes for infants, is tending to rediscover its special character.

9

To be christian
is to be baptised
in the faith of the Church

Once received into the Church

A person has been received into the Church. People have come to join the christians.

They have been presented by parents, relatives, a sponsoring group.

They are not baptised. Not yet. But they are already part of the Church, even if it is still to a limited extent.

Are they going to stop in this state which normally is one of transition? Nobody can say precisely. They themselves not always. But what is certain is that they can find in the Church the taste and the desire for going further. That they can expect. It is their due. For they know well enough if they are adults, or even children already aware, their initiation is not at an end.

If they prolong their initial request and wish to continue along the road,[1] the means offered them before their entry into the Church are to be presented to them again. They are the same, basically: the Word of God, dialogue with christians, deepening of their relations with those around them, catechesis. However there are some apparent differences. One stage has been covered and from now on they are going to go forward within the Church, in close solidarity with the christians. And then other ceremonies will be set before them in which the ardent strength of faith will be expressed.

The initiation rituals lay stress on two essential factors at this point in the advance: they indicate a need to listen again and always to the Word of God and to enter into the spiritual struggle which cannot fail to attend upon anyone wishing to be more profoundly converted. The baptismal rite for adults adds a third reality which

1. The ritual for children of school age (French edition) suggests the following formula: "Now I believe in Jesus; I can make the sign of the cross. With you I want to continue learning to be a child of God; with you I want to do what Jesus asks". This declaration which appears towards the end of the Church reception takes in practice the place of the 'election' addressed to the adult catechumens (but its significance is obviously different).

it presents as 'of great concern': the catechumens hear themselves called by the Church to go forward to the sacraments of initiation.

To be initiated is to be called
to the sacraments of faith

Let us begin by emphasising what is represented by the 'election', by their christian names, of the adult catechumens. I have already said a few words on this in the previous chapter since something of this celebration in the Middle Ages slipped into the liturgy of entry into the Church for infants. This 'call' is reserved today to adults preparing for baptism.

This is how the rite for adults presents this act which takes place at the beginning of Lent, often in the presence of the bishop: "When Lent comes, the final call is celebrated. It can be considered as the turning point in the whole catechumenate. In this rite, the Church hears the testimony of those of her members acting as sponsors and catechists, and the affirmation by the catechumens of their will to receive the sacraments" (French edition).[1] Three roles consequently: that of the christians accompanying or presenting the candidates and who are therefore in the position of godparents: that of the people to be baptised; that of the community as a whole united around the bishop. The ritual continues: "In the name of the Church, the bishop or his delegate takes note of the state of preparation of the catechumens and signifies to them that they may approach the sacraments".[1] Two aspects therefore: what has been and what will be. The request which was made is taken up by the Church, who transforms it into a call on her part addressed to those wishing to become christians. The rite combining these two intentions is for them to 'give their names' by enrolling or signing their names in a register, 'the book of the elect'.

It could well be that in the 4th-5th centuries, at Jerusalem or in Rome, this rite at first had a practical application: people signed up for the coming sacramental celebrations. But this process meant re-expressing the request for initiation formulated before. It was a sign that the initial request, while it had evolved, was still present, and was now to be based on life in the Church. Very soon the liturgy gave this rite a new significance. It is the Church who officially, through the bishop, calls to the sacraments those wishing to receive them. There is here a kind of reversal of the position of the cate-chumens. They are certainly asking. But the Church too asks them to complete their initiation. She needs them as they need her.

1. See 'The Rites', Introductory notes, 23.
2. Introductory notes, French version, 4.05.

A contingent rite

Why is this ceremony not included in every christian initiation? Why does it come into adult initiation only? Quite simply because its two complementary meanings, the request by the catechumens and the call from the Church, are not discernible except in the case of an initiation celebrated in distinct liturgical stages dependent on Lent and Easter, and at least in theory in the presence of the bishop. When conditions for such a programme of initiation do not occur, when the rite becomes cut off from Lent and Easter and is celebrated in the absence of the bishop, it is understandable that it is difficult to maintain the celebration of the election. For it is under the heading of the liturgical seasons and presupposes the presence of the bishop or his delegate.

Neither does the 'condensed' liturgy used for infant baptism keep the rite of election. It recapitulates however several celebrations which for adults are separate in time. For example the welcome to the church and the rite of baptism itself. But for the rite of election it was hardly possible to integrate it as it was. There is therefore substituted the question on the christian name during the reception liturgy.

As for the ritual for school-age children, it has not retained the rite of election by the Church, either. For precisely the same reasons as the infant rite. On looking closely at the liturgy provided for older children it is possible doubtless to see here likewise traces of this suppressed ceremony. There is first of all the initial stage, before the reception, consisting of the official registration of the request for baptism made by the child. There is certainly account made there of the progress to be undertaken. But if there is a registration, it does not bear directly on the christian name and above all it cannot at this stage of the progression have the two significances of the 'final call' meant for adults, that is a reformulation of the initial request and the link established between the desire on the part of the catechumen and the coming call from the Church. We might again find in one of the formulas of commitment suggested in connection with the ceremony of reception into the Church something of an equivalent to the advance implied by the ceremony of election addressed to adults. But here again there is an alteration in the meaning.

The style of initiation

If I am going into some detail over the rite of election and its hazards, this is because the liturgical action is here symptomatic and expresses rather well certain features of christian initiation.

Notice first of all that during initiation, the mystery of the christian faith can be more or less expounded. In some cases one or other aspect is emphasised which is not brought out on another occasion. In practice not all initiation includes the rite of election. Whatever may be the reasons for this variation, it appears to me to constitute in itself a notable fact.

Next, I should like to point out that initiation links two dimensions, the one more personal, the other more objective or institutional. The election is the imparting of ecclesial objectivity to the personal advance of the catechumens. This is signalled by suiting the ceremony to the liturgical calendar (they 'go through' Lent, will be baptised at Easter), and by the presence of the head of the local Church, the bishop. These elements are not however considered entirely indispensable.

That can be understood, certainly, in reference to the bishop, who from the time when baptisms became very frequent in the West and were given individually, could not be personally at all the initiation ceremonies. But the connection with the calendar appears, at least in theory, to keep a certain importance. I mean that the rituals allude to it. The ritual for adults indicates that the baptismal celebration for adults should take account of it: "The election therefore normally takes place at the beginning of Lent and the sacraments of initiation on the Vigil of Easter or during Eastertide"[1]. For its part, the ritual for infants declares: "To bring out the paschal character of baptism, it is recommended that the sacraments be celebrated during the Easter Vigil or on Sunday, when the Church commemorates the Lord's resurrection"[2]. As for the ritual for children of school age it does not raise the problem, preferring to stress solely the spiritual journey of the catechumens, which to my mind is a pity.[3]

Finally, you see perhaps there is the problem in the western tradition of bringing in the bishop, not only after baptism for the sacrament of confirmation but also before the actual baptism, for the election. There is here something to put us on our guard against those interpretations of christian initiation which make excessive distinctions between the 'speciality' or significance of various points in the process. Certainly the bishop enters in after the baptism. But he

1. 'The Rites', Introductory notes, 111 A, 51 and B, 58.
2. Introductory note, 9.
3. No. 10 in the French version of the Introductory is content with noting that "the dates for the celebration of the various stages cannot be fixed *a priori*, as it is fitting that each one should correspond in fact to the child's progress in the faith and that of the group". Should not this rider apply also to adults? And yet for them Easter-time customarily offers a manifest symbolic value (see Introductory notes, 20.310).

also enters in before it. And similar examples of this type can be easily multiplied: reference to the Holy Spirit not reserved to the ceremony of confirmation, the gesture of imposition of hands repeated on several occasions throughout initiation, likewise the sign of the cross.

What does this indicate? It signifies that initiation is not solely linear but continually brings before us the same realities, while each time revealing them in a new light. It means also that the purport of the various moments in initiation is to gain an understanding of it not only from the symbolic actions of the liturgy or the words pronounced but also from their position in the whole sequence.

The Word evangelises and liberates

New believers have been received into the Church and have begun to discover church life from the inside. In practice they have met the same realities as those with which they had previously been initiated. But they appreciate them differently. Then if they are adults they were called by the Church. And if they are very small the celebration of their reception will be extended with a view to the sacramental celebration.

What next?

The liturgy of initiation provides a fairly characteristic celebration in which the evangelising Word of God is put to work, with its liberating power to aid those asking for baptism in the spiritual struggle which the faith arouses in them.

In the ritual for infants the intervention of the Word of God is not obvious, for in fact, as a result of the compacting of the rites, it is merged with that ending the reception ceremony. But this intervention has its full place in what the western liturgical tradition calls, with a word which sounds weird yet meaningful, the 'scrutinies'.

By this is meant the ceremonies — normally during Lent — in the course of which the assembly invokes the God who 'scrutinises the reins and the hearts' (Rev 2,23) to enlighten those who are to be baptised and free them from sin. Formerly the ceremonies brought christians and catechumens together. All were there associated in the same penitential course. And this was in line with the scriptural texts announcing God's pardon and gift. Three gospel passages are indeed traditionally linked with the conversion recommended in Lent: the gospel of the Samaritan woman (the water of life), the account of the healing of the man born blind (light), the passage telling of the raising of Lazarus (the mystery of life overcoming death).

Of great importance is the accent on the saving power the Word of God has in us. The baptismal liturgy stresses this traditionally and in all the rituals.[1] But the link between liberation from evil and the Divine Word is not perhaps always sufficiently appreciated. The impression is sometimes given that the liturgy of the Word is followed by the prayer for deliverance from sin and the rite of exorcism without any effective co-operation between the two rites. The movement is in fact not very obvious in the ritual for infants. But the liturgy of the 'scrutinies' for adults is perfectly clear on this point. The priest prefaces the prayer leading to the prayer of exorcism by speaking on one or other of the three gospel passages to which I have just alluded. It is not merely a teaching device. It is an affirmation of the faith in God who saves today as yesterday. Today is made real what took place once before. Baptism makes remembrance of the gospel liberations.

You can see therefore, the Word of God expresses the actual presence of the mystery. At the same time it gathers together in the same faith those who are already baptised and those who are going to be baptised. Both groups are together listening to one and the same unique Word. All are called to conversion. So much so that the baptised are a sign to those who are not baptised: they are still faced with evil and have not finished with sin. Conversely the catechumens by their presence declare that the baptised are called daily to make present in their lives the Gospel of deliverance and the baptism into freedom which they have received.

In addition, the Word of God puts us in a state of prayer, before arousing an attitude of penitence. Here we have the logic of the Gospel. This is especially clear in the baptismal progression followed by adults. Once entered officially on the catechumenate, having been received and marked with the sign of the cross, they are at once publicly invited to listen to Scripture and to pray. They have not to wait to do this, since from then on they have been brought into the ambient of the church. Christian initiation shows the path of faith: reception by the Church leads to the Word, the Word leads to prayer and, in the fulness of time, this brings deliverance.

Baptismal deliverance

This deliverance, baptism signifies in very realistic fashion. At this point, baptism is indeed initiating, for it manifests exactly what evil and sin are and what forgiveness and liberation. It must however be realised that in this area, always a difficult one, it is not infant baptism which speaks most clearly. It will be to our interest in order

---

1. The liturgy of the Reformed Church showed itself aware earlier than the Roman liturgy of a certain need for discretion in an area of mystery, more often piously imagined than understood according to faith.

to grasp the significance of baptism to take account of the three
present Roman rituals together.

Stress is laid first of all on the understanding the catechumens need
and which they must ask of God. In the ritual for adults that is made
plain: "Free them from the spirit of falsehood and help them to
recognise any evil within themselves", "free your chosen ones from
the falsehood that surrounds and blinds them".

Next, sin, deliverance from which in Jesus Christ is evidenced by
baptism, is recognised under its various forms. The three gospels of
the scrutinies describe it concretely as weakness without a guide (the
Samaritan woman), a state of darkness (the man born blind) and the
works or the situation of death (raising of Lazarus).

Third aspect: baptism, which is a radical renewal, takes issue with
evil and sin in what they too have which is radical. In a certain
sense they precede our free-will. They are in existence before us.
Hence the two complementary figures of original sin and the devil.
The one and the other speak in two different ways, the negative that
is 'there first' before human existence and which we uncover when
Jesus delivers us from it.[1]

Fourth feature: deliverance is in principle possible at any age, for
the hold over us of evil and even of sin is not connected with our
legal standing, it affects human nature to its depths, which is to say
from its beginnings. In other words the newly-born and adults have
in common that they belong to the same handicapped state, granted
admittedly that they do not take it on in the same way.

Finally, fifth indication: sin, which is a sickness of freedom and
of faith, is never named in the Church except with regard to God's
working to free human beings from it. Hence in the rituals the
insistence on Christ's light and power, or again on the Holy Spirit.[2]

Thus understood, baptismal liberation requires to be expressed in
symbol. Several rites have been or are possible. First of all, the most
ancient, already found in the 'Apostolic Tradition' of Hippolytus, the

---

1. The passages suggested for the scrutinies in the ritual for adults do not
speak of original sin but only of Satan or the spirit of evil. The ritual for
school-children equally mentions only the spirit of darkness. It is therefore
only the rite for infants which speaks both of Satan and of original sin. The
differences in style are remarkable. Is this a sign of the considerable difficulty
found today in conceiving of original sin? Perhaps. Is it not also a sign
that the classic concept of original sin is linked with the newly-born? It
no longer impinges for children of school age or for adults, even when we
recognise the radical nature of sin and evil by experience.

2. In the exorcisms forming part of the scrutinies, prayer is made at two
points. It is addressed to God. Then it turns to Jesus who is addressed
directly which is unusual in the Roman liturgy. And it is when speaking to
Jesus that mention is made of the Holy Spirit.

imposition of hands. Or again another rite, also going back to the 3rd century, anointing with oil signifying the necessary strength to fight against evil, from which God delivers us certainly but which we still must continue to resist. The ritual for infants as revised in 1969 gives a choice between these two rites.[1] And most often it is the imposition of hands which is used. For adult baptism the exorcisms are accompanied by the same gesture. But the anointing remains a possibility as a special rite on the eve of baptism.

The present tendency in the West is to reduce the diversity of rites. One gesture has, besides, been recently suppressed, that of lightly breathing on the catechumens as a sign of their new creation and the coming of the Holy Spirit.[2] For adult initiation the 'ephetha' rite is now optional.[3]

Water of faith

Christian initiation comprises firstly a reception brought to a close with the sign of the cross, then a liturgy of the Word ending with a rite of deliverance. It is now time to come to the central action, combining the rite of water and the commitment in faith.

First the water is blessed. This blessing is of ancient origin. It forms part of a tradition going back perhaps to the 3rd century,[4] and has been maintained in the West as in the East.[5] It had disappeared from the ritual for infant baptism. It was brought back by the 1969 revision. It has gradually found a place in the ritual of baptism for older children. As for adults, it comes in quite normally, under the same form as in the Paschal Vigil, since it is indeed the paschal liturgy which has borrowed the formula from the baptismal liturgy.

The water to be used for the baptismal rite is therefore linked with salvation history. It is put under the aegis of the Holy Spirit and signed with the cross of Christ. It is a water of purification signalling the ontological gulf that exists between the creature and God. But it is also a water of remembrance, making real the sacred history of God's dealings with humanity. A water of hope and certainly witnessing to God's forgiveness of human sin. And it is a spiritual water

---

1. This is also possible in the case of children of school age.
2. The liturgies of the East have ordinarily kept it. Until 1969 it had a place in the Roman ritual.
3. This section, recalling Mk 7,34, is a repeat of the welcome into the Church and evokes the opening up of the whole being to the faith.
4. Augustine alludes to it. An Ethiopian version of the 'Apostolic Tradition' gives a version of it. Lastly, Cyprian writes: "The water must first be purified and sanctified by the priest so as to be able to wash away sins" (Letter 70, no. 1).
5. The Lutheran and Reformed Churches omit it however, for fear of giving too much importance to the material element of water.

which transmits the life of the paschal mystery.

Consequently there is here no inept positivism which would insist on the material element of water to the detriment of faith. It is a water of faith which baptism employs. A water distilled in faith exactly so that baptism shall be clearly seen for what it is, a gospel action in the Spirit.

Faith declared

Then comes the profession of faith. After being expressed by water, faith is put into words. With the twofold aspect characterising this affirmation knowingly made: renunciation and adherence. The renunciation extends the act of deliverance performed earlier.[1] And this is easy to understand. It is not possible to be freed from evil and the spirit of evil except in so far as, thanks be to God, their seductiveness is renounced. In other words, renunciation of what is contrary to the Spirit, and this is evil, is a first effect of the liberation asked of God and received from his Holy Spirit. The adherence expresses faith in the Triune God in whom the believers hope. This adherence is built around their relationship with Christ. That is emphasised in the syrian, coptic and byzantine rites.[2]

What to me seems significant in this connection is the linking of no and yes. Is this not always the way for christians? The faith we so often query nowadays does not appear either as an unqualified refusal nor simply as an affirmative. It consists in breaking with ways of living to which we cannot subscribe and at the same time offering adherence to the Gospel which liberates and makes new.[3]

At the same time, notice that the profession of faith under its two connected aspects is formulated in question-and-answer form. The West has kept this old tradition, unlike the East. We are perhaps accustomed to this ritual since it is taken up every year by the Paschal Vigil. But as such it certainly marks an aspect of the faith not as clearly indicated by the Credo alone. To believe, indeed, is not to look within oneself for words or gestures of faith. It is to take a decision after being aroused to it by others and in particular being drawn to it by the christian tradition.

1. However, in the 3rd century the 'Apostolic Tradition' places the oil of deliverance after the renunciation as though to complete it. This is still the custom in the byzantine rite. The western arrangement is no less expressive.

2. Byzantine rite: "Do you join yourself to Christ? I join myself to him. — Are you joined to Christ? I am joined to him".

3. The eastern rites multiply the symbolism here. The byzantine rite requires a renunciation of the spirit of evil while turning towards the west, that is to the setting sun, with an explicit sign of contempt. Adherence to Christ is then made by turning towards the east, the rising sun.

Of course in the case of little children this expression of faith leaves something of a gap. For it is in their own name that adults take their stand. The new ritual does not here try to conceal the surprising part in the practice of infant baptism. Therefore it is plain that one person cannot believe in place of another. But it is also shown that the faith of the Church must be expressed at the baptism of a baby if the child is one day to make it its own.

The water of baptism

The water prepared and the faith confessed, the baptism with water can proceed. The priest pours the water three times over the head of those presented for baptism, naming each of them by name and saying: "I baptise you in the name of the Father and of the Son and of the Holy Spirit".

The people present are sometimes excessively drawn to this particular moment.[1] A little like at the consecration of the Mass in former times. In fact, in the same way as the eucharistic consecration is not to be separated from the whole celebration, so the rite of water cannot be dissociated from the confession of faith which precedes it and the actions which will follow.

This close relationship between the water of baptism and sacramental faith was formerly more clearly marked than today. In the 3rd century each of the three questions on the faith was followed by the *Amen* of the catechumen and immediately by a pouring of the water.[2] The sacramental form had therefore not the same words as at present. Today a Latin priest declares: "I baptise you in the name of the Father and of the Son and of the Holy Spirit". This formula did not exist. For it was the dialogue between ministers and believer which constituted the sacramental form.

In any case, in all the liturgical traditions the action of baptising has a trinitarian sense and is performed by a minister. A person is baptised in the name of the Triune God. And we do not baptise ourselves.

1. It is still clearer where total immersion of infants is practised in the baptismal laver. The practice is traditional in the East. The Roman rituals keep it as a possibility.
2. This is the surprising testimony of Hippolytus: that the one who is to receive baptism "goes down into the water and the one who is baptising him places his hand on him saying: 'Do you believe in God the all-powerful Father?' And the one being baptised replies: 'I do believe'. Let him baptise him once, keeping his hand on his head. Then let him say: 'Do you believe in Christ Jesus, the Son of God. . . ?' And when he has said 'I do believe', let him baptise him again. Let him say again: 'Do you believe in the Holy Spirit, in Holy Church, and in the resurrection of the body?' Let him who is baptised say: 'I believe'. And so let him be baptised a third time" (no. 21).

The triple action performed with the water symbolises indeed not only the faith in its three main articles but more profoundly God's own commitment as Father, Son and Holy Spirit. Receiving baptism is therefore to receive into one's life the very life of God, into one's name as a human being the threefold divine name, into one's existence the mysterious efficacy of this mysterious name of the Trinity. Being baptised is therefore not only believing in God, it is being united vitally with him, merging one's life in him. By the act of baptism, God integrates a person into the movement of his Word working in the world. It makes someone who is already received into the Church enter into the gospel tradition by communicating what I have already at the beginning of this book called faith-memory. From now on the baptised person is truly in a position to be a witness to Christ and to make remembrance of him by actualising his presence. That is how it is since the commencement of Matthew 28,19: "baptise them in the name of the Father and of the Son and of the Holy Spirit".

What in this context is the significance of the counterpart to the one being baptised, this minister of the Church who intervenes in the baptismal ceremony? It is not necessarily a priest. It could be a deacon. But in principle in the christian tradition it is a qualified minister of importance. Since the 3rd century certain polemics of which Tertullian gives us the echo shows that the problem had been debated.[1] In urgent cases any baptised person can confer baptism. "Baptism (which is) a gift of God can be given by all", affirms Tertullian. But it is understood, given the ecclesial value of the sacrament, that the Church's ministry is part of the ceremony at once in its diversity and in its effective reality. The eastern tradition is very firm on this point. So are the Reformed Churches.[2] The Lutherans and the Catholics have maintained the exception of urgent cases. Vatican II, in a phrase which is not of the happiest, even notes that "any believer can baptise".

It appears to me that the problem raised by the role of the minister in the celebration of baptism is less sensitive today than that raised by his intervention in other forms of church life. It is understood indeed that baptism involves the Church and therefore calls for an explicit manifestation from her of what she is. The ordained minister contributes to this image of the Church.

But for this there are several conditions. First of all, ministry in the Church is collegial. In Antiquity it was neither the bishops nor

1. Tertullian, De Baptismo, 17.
2. Lumen Gentium, 17. See for a more detailed reference the introduction to the ritual for baptism of 1969, 11–17.

usually the priests who baptised, but the deacons. And it was done in the communion of the Church and the whole assembly of ministers. Consequently, we can conceive of lay people with a precise, recognised function, notably in preparation for baptism, being able to preside at the celebration of baptism in union with the ordained ministers. On the other hand the ministers of the baptismal act should not be reverenced. They are themselves at the service of the mystery and their role cannot be fulfilled without a concrete relationship with the assembly. They are not alone in celebrating the baptism. They preside in the midst of the people. And they act in the name of God. For it is God who baptises after all. Besides, this is what marks the baptismal formula used in many eastern Churches: "Such a one is baptised". I have already alluded to this passive construction which answers to the active form in the western Churches: "I baptise you".[1]

*   *   *

Summary

What shall we take, from the point of view of initiation, from the periods and celebrations extending from reception into the Church to baptism?

— Firstly, the fact that life in the Church, begun with the sign of the cross, is deepened through a *struggle* or fight. As though a kind of 'mystagogia' gradually brought out the deepest implications in belonging to the Church.

— But at the same time the catechumens find in the Church the assurance that God is committed to his people. The spiritual combat referred to leads to say no to the false names of alienating powers, idols and the spirit of evil, ends in victory and deliverance, because of the Holy Spirit of Jesus Christ.

— To be baptised is therefore to commit oneself in God's regard in a new way, *given that* God commits himself in regard to those he calls to the sacraments of initiation. It means being born again, receiving the holy name of God and bearing it thenceforward along with one's own name.

1. Chrysostom (end of the 4th century): "The priest does not say: I baptise N. but: N. is baptised, showing by this that he is only a servant of grace, contenting himself with being an instrument, because it is for this work that he has been ordained on the part of the Spirit" (Second Baptismal Catechesis, 26). Theodore of Mopsuestia (same period): "He does not say: I baptise, but: is baptised. No, not a man exists capable of such a gift. Divine grace alone can achieve it" (Third Homily on Baptism, 16).

— The reality of the Church, so obscured sometimes today, is thus shown to the baptised in quite a precise fashion. The Church has already revealed her identity in receiving the catechumens. By baptising them she appears as the people God establishes and charges to *make remembrance* of Christ in the world. We are indeed baptised 'in the faith of the Church' as the traditional augustinian formula has it.

— This Church of baptism is therefore a Church which hands on the Gospel from the beginning, in other words tradition, an act of remembrance. She is equally a Church greater than the small group gathered for the ceremony, even though this group is the tangible, indispensable, symbol of the total mystery. Finally, the Church of baptism presents herself as an integral part of the baptised's advance. The catechumen's request is united with the Church's call.

— I would add that the *sacrament of baptism* is a remembrance of Christ, memorial of the paschal mystery. First of all because the name of the Trinity is invoked in the Church as she now is. Next because the Church, the sacramental body of Christ, is committed in the sacramental act. Finally, because the rite of baptism brings into one, as does all memorial, a symbolic action, words, the expression of personal and essential faith, the commitment of God himself.

— The *developing process* of christian initiation introduces successively certain symbolic gestures expressive of the mystery of faith. At the moment of reception into the Church it is the marking with the cross which is the important sign. Next, at the moment of the election there is the commitment of the individual by name, christian name. Then, with the liturgy of deliverance comes in the gesture of laying on of hands. Finally, in the act of baptism itself the key action is the water being poured over the body. Yet all these various symbols are linked with a continuity, the presence of the Church. This Church surrounds and accompanies the initiates at the same time as confronting them. She communicates to them the Word of God in whose service she sees herself to be, in prayer and in hope.

— Finally, I should like to emphasise the *penitential aspect* taken by christian initiation in the ceremonies we have been going through. Often this aspect makes for difficulty. Many find that baptism is too often presented as bound up with sin, especially in regard to infant baptism. I do not contradict this estimation. But it appears to me that the liturgy of initiation has a more sensitive way of looking at sin than is often said. It speaks of it as a fundamental reality which does not even require an exact confession on the part of the initiates, it is so obviously an element of christian experience as seen through the spiritual combat in the life of a believer.

— It is clear none the less that this penitential aspect is a *delicate matter*. It does not take much for it to founder under pessimistic interpretations of human existence or to engender imaginary guilt. Understanding of baptism in the West has not been free of these dangers. The water has become principally a water of purification, when it is above all the water of spiritual holiness and hope.

10

To be christian
is to continue
initiation after baptism

It's not all over

The faith has been confessed beside the spiritual water of baptism. And that water has flowed over those who, already received by the Church, thus became an active part of the christian baptismal movement in the world and in their own daily lives.

Christian initiation is not completed, though.

Here are some ancient texts which are very clear on this point. First of all Cyprian, bishop of Carthage in the 3rd century: "It is necessary for the one who has been baptised to be signed with oil: receiving the oil, that is the anointing, he can thus be the anointed of God and have in him the grace of Christ".[1] Or again: "Those who have been baptised in the Church are presented to the leaders of the Church . . . so as to be made complete by the sign of the Lord".[2] In the 4th century Cyril, bishop of Jerusalem: "Admitted to this holy anointing you are called christians and your regeneration justified the name. Before receiving that grace you did not properly merit that title. You were only on the way to becoming christian".[3] At the same period in the West, Ambrose, bishop of Milan: "After the font, it still remains to be brought to completion, when at the invocation of the bishop the Holy Spirit is poured out".[4]

These passages are enough to grasp the traditional belief.[5] We are not christian by baptism alone. Rather, in the etymological sense the word christian, which evokes Christ, refers to him in the mystery of his divine identity, sealed by the presence of the Spirit: to be

1. Letter 70.2,2: Cyprian takes pleasure in comparing the anointed christian and the anointed of God, Christ. Anointed and Christ both mean in fact 'marked with oil'. By the anointing the christian is therefore christed, christened.

2. Letter 73.9,2: Complete has here the sense of plenitude: the anointing makes christians complete.

3. Mystagogical catechesis 3,1.5.

4. Of the Sacraments 3,8.

5. It should be pointed out however that the need to expound baptism was not felt in one of the ancient Churches, the Syrian.

christian is to be anointed with the spiritual unction borne by Christ.

It appears to me useful to say this again today for we sometimes have the tendency to place too much reliance on baptism. Wrongly, for to do so makes impossible an initiation celebrated in several acts. The infant just baptised but not yet confirmed and not yet given Communion is "on the way to becoming christian" as Cyril of Jerusalem expresses it. Not yet 'a complete christian'.

Consequently, after the baptism ceremony, other celebrations are still on the 'programme' of initiation. We have to assimilate what has happened to us so as to take in the full meaning. And then it is time to approach the table of the eucharist around which are grouped the people of the baptised.

Assimilating the meaning of the baptism ceremony

It is not that the first celebration has recourse to simply complementary secondary moments. It is truly initiation continuing. In other words, the rite of water, however powerfully symbolic it may be, does not focus on itself the whole of initiation, not even all its baptismal significances. It would therefore be wrong to take it in isolation. Just as initiation begins before it, so it goes on after it.

Here there is a principle of diversification in ritual which is rather important. In initiation, one rite on its own cannot do everything, say everything, for what is initiated is a process.

In practice the present Roman rituals preserve what has been gradually developed in the history of the West. Four ceremonies follow after the rite of water: an anointing with oil, the clothing with the white garment, the giving of the lighted candle, a laying on of hands. The recent revision of the Latin liturgy has not changed this arrangement. It has however introduced two new elements. On the one hand it has made optional, for adults and children of school age, the white garment. On the other hand, in cases where the eucharist is not celebrated at once, consequently for infant baptism, it has introduced four rites which are provisional concluding rites to the baptism ceremony: the participants go up to the altar towards the eucharist that is to come, they say the Lord's Prayer, the parents and the assembly receive a blessing, finally they take up a thanksgiving chant.

Where the rites have varied

It can be seen the diversification is broad. The recent reform made further additions. Besides, 'paraliturgical' rites, dear to popular faith, are sometimes again joined on to the series. For example, in France the traditional presentation of the newborn child to Our Lady. Or again the distribution of dragees:[1] the newly-baptised taste — or at least are invited to taste — the food of the messianic kingdom, milk and honey, before they come to the eucharist.[2] In the course of history this variety was besides sometimes even greater. Thus in the Milanese liturgy at the end of the 4th century, the bishop washed the feet of the newly-baptised adults[3] thus making remembrance of Jesus' action on the evening of Maundy Thursday.

This diversification of rites, sometimes a little quaint, is not without charm. Hard not to feel this in an age such as ours, somewhat dominated by austerity in matters of ritual. But it has the danger of drowning the essential under a multiplicity of exuberant gestures. Perhaps also, rather than inducing acceptance, it risks the initiation being enervated by illustrations of the realities of the faith. It is this tendency to allegory which is seen in the rite of the white garment, attested in the West from the 4th century[4] and also that of giving a candle, which appears in the Roman liturgy between the 9th to the 12th centuries. Finally, one last encumbrance, the diversification of postbaptismal rites leads not only to a shift of meaning between one and another but also in the East to a surprising doublet, a strange repetition: the anointing with oil is given twice, at two separate points: I shall return to this.[5]

Furthermore, the taste for diversification of the rites following baptism is not a universal norm. It is characteristic of the Roman ritual and also, fairly widely, of the eastern rituals. But it is under suspicion in the Churches descended from the Reform.

In the Churches of the East, the conclusion to baptism consists as in the West, in an anointing with oil which completes the rite of water. It is customarily multiplied in several signs over the body of the newly-

1. Les dragées de baptême — sugared almonds or other small sweets sent round to relatives and friends rather as in our custom with wedding cake.

2. In the 3rd century Tertullian seems to be already alluding to this custom; cf. Contra Marcion 1,14.3.

3. Ambrose of Milan, De sacramentis, III 4–7. St Ambrose is definite: "We are not unaware that the Roman Church has not this custom". And he comments: "I desire to follow the Roman Church in all things. But we too have some good sense".

4. This rite gives an allegorical significance to what was at first a quite practical and functional action, dressing again after the rite of water. It is to be found today . . . less commonly used, since only the ritual for infants gives it as a norm and the other rituals as optional. To me it appears interesting however to note that, in France, women presenting themselves for baptism often choose, and without being told, to dress in white or to wear a white shawl.

5. But for the moment I think it a better method not so separate what we call the end of baptism from confirmation. Continuity here is more important than to distinguish between them.

baptised.[1] Sometimes, but not always, the unction is accompanied, as is the case in the West for the second postbaptismal anointing (that called confirmation) by a laying on of the hand or hands. Except in the byzantine ritual, the anointing ends with a remarkable gesture unknown in the West, a rite of coronation. This action finds its functional origin in the band round the head to absorb any excess oil, lavishly poured on the head of the baptised person. It has taken on allegorical significance in a similar way to that of the white garment or the candle in the West.

In the Reformed Churches the rituals, which are variable, have in common that they do not multiply gestures tending to obscure the essential act of the mystery and the faith. This restraint, which indeed is the mark of the whole liturgy of initiation in these Churches, is especially clear at the end of the baptism ceremony. The Lutherans make a sign of the cross on the forehead of the newly-baptised. The Free Churches usually practise imposition of hands and often place here the obligations of the parents towards the child.

Taking pleasure in diversity

All the same it appears to me that the diversity of the rites following on the rite of baptism in most of the liturgical traditions is clearly of some interest in spite of the dangers I have indicated.

First of all, let me repeat, this diversification prevents a misplaced reverential attitude towards the rite of water.

Next, by reason of its richness, the conclusion to the baptism ceremony slowly became settled in diversity. There resulted a transference of meaning between the gestures or between the accompanying words. This did not simplify their task for liturgists and theologians, who sometimes would like to identify distinct 'effects' to be imputed to this or that precise action. But it does after all serve initiation. When meanings are fluid, when different co-ordinations can be established between symbols, that is evocative. For mystery will not allow itself to be detailed out into elements which are autonomous and plainly distinct. And it is useless to try to attribute a specific 'effect' to each action taken in isolation.

I would add that the diversity of postbaptismal acts seems to me to produce a type-experience. It is a question in fact of adopting what has been done up to this point during the process of initiation and notably by the rite of water. But how is that to be expressed in a single fashion? How integrate the plurality of christian attitudes and expectations? The diversification of the postbaptismal rites translates to my mind the plurality of christian experience. It expresses the multiple dimensions of faith undergoing baptism.

1. The ancient Syrian Church however did not possess this rite.

A commentary directed towards the future

Yet this diversity is not meaningless. It is centred on the time to come. And that is why I am glad the postbaptismal rites are as much turned towards the future of faith as towards the past of initiation already accomplished.

This orientation towards the future is expressed in two ways.

First in terms of *eschatological hope*: "Bring it unstained to the judgment seat of our Lord Jesus Christ so that you may have everlasting life", says the celebrant presiding at an adult baptism when giving the white garment.[1] "When the Lord comes, may you go out to meet him with all the saints in the heavenly kingdom", he says next when giving the paschal light.[2] Notice that this hope is not unmindful of the weakness of the newly-baptised: they must guard the baptismal state they have received and go forward as children of light.[3]

Next, the direction of the postbaptismal rites converges on the *eucharist*. This is an ancient fact which the western liturgy traditionally signifies by the kiss of peace given to adults newly baptised, before celebrating the eucharist with them.[4] It is the equivalent of our present kiss of peace preserved in the confirmation ceremony, and therefore associated with it: this gesture with its eucharistic sense was formerly inappropriately interpreted as a blow symbolising the struggles of faith. The ritual for confirmation published in 1971 replaces this with other gestures more suited to the contemporary mentality. But these gestures retain basically a eucharistic reference directed to the reception of communion.

This bearing is emphasised in the recent reform of the Roman ritual where the celebration of baptism does not go straight on into the eucharistic celebration, as is the practice in infant baptism. To give baptism to the newborn is certainly not to ignore the main eschatological dimension of the baptismal action, by the very reason of the opening onto the future implied by such a gesture.[5] But the baptismal liturgy for infants, as it is now revised, emphasises that baptism, in order to make towards the end of time and eternal life, should ordinarily pass on to the eucharist. This is the significance of the procession to the altar. And

1. The formula is almost the same in the ritual for school-age children. Infant baptism is content with mentioning eternal life.

2. The same turn of expression, practically, in the three rituals.

3. On coming out of the water. And this is where the prospect of possible falling away is evoked. This is the real baptismal hope: it is hope in a Kingdom granted to sinners in forgiveness.

4. The eastern liturgies, notably the coptic, emphasise the eucharistic orientation, starting with the blessing of the water: the prayer of this blessing is a parallel to the eucharistic prayer.

5. The new ritual also signals this feature with the blessing of the parents and those present, at the end of the postbaptismal rites.

this is also indicated by the Lord's Prayer said by all present. This rite is of ancient origin. But formerly it came in at the close of the baptism ceremony. In the African liturgy of St Augustine it was placed during Lent before baptism.[1] And it remained at this point in initiation for centuries. Thereafter, following on the rite of water, it anticipates the Lord's Prayer of the eucharist. So it is made clear that baptism demands prayer, the ultimate form of it being the eucharist.[2]

Taking up the same gestures
and beginning again

The diversification of the ritual which interprets and extends the rite of water acts therefore as 'mystagogia'. It is borne along by the dynamic of initiation.

Note that diversification does not necessarily mean employing improvised gestures. After the baptism itself there are certainly new rites not used earlier in the liturgy. Such are presenting the white garment and the candle. Or the procession to the altar, the recitation of the Lord's Prayer and the blessing of the parents and those present during infant baptism. Or the Lord's Prayer and the kiss of peace. Or again, finally, the eucharistic celebration. But others of the rites had already been included in the initiation. Here they are again, bearers now of deeper meaning. This is the case with the anointing.[3] It is also the case with the sign of the cross: it is repeated over the baptised after having been made over them at the ceremony of entry into the Church. Going further, we might even reckon the rite of blessing in more than one part of the rite of water to be a repetition if we accept to take together the blessing of the baptismal water and that of those present at infant baptism.[4] In the same way, before and after the rite of water, baptismal hope is ex-

1. The Lord's Prayer was given to the catechumens at the same time as the Creed. And then, putting to work the christian faculty of memory developed in them by initiation, they recited these two texts.
2. The Creed did no undergo the same history. For a long time associated with the Lord's Prayer, it was not displaced along with it. Which is easily understood. For, if there are meaningful doublets, this one constituted by the recitation of the Creed before the interrogations on the faith in the Trinity scarcely justified its inclusion in the one ceremony. It was therefore suppressed.
3. The postbaptismal anointing with oil has a prebaptismal counterpart, an anointing which in the Roman rite for a long time accompanied the rite of deliverance. It was made with the oil called 'oil of catechumens'. Today it has become optional. But in the eastern rites this prebaptismal anointing remains very important.
4. As an extreme example a third blessing could be found in the liturgy of initiation if we take the reception into the Church with the sign of the cross accompanying it as a form of blessing, which would be all the more plain if the celebration of the child's christian name were to be accompanied by a blessing given by the parents.

pressed, in the consciousness of human frailty, yet certain of the coming of the Kingdom.

What is the meaning of this 'repetition' of symbols already used? It indicates, it appears to me, that christian initiation is not linear, in the sense that the candidates would go from discovery to discovery exploring new territory. Christianity initiates by making us go back again over what we have once perceived, making us deepen what has already been experienced. Obviously new things are interspersed along the way: the rite of water is one. But the newness operates in a continuity. And it is in this gradually deepening continuity that can be found the basis of christian remembrance and what is called 'anamnesis' or memorial.

Interpretation Christ-centred

The problem, then, is to show what requires to be taken up again or deepened once the rite of water has been celebrated.

The preceding considerations allow of advancing some elements of a reply.

If, in the postbaptismal rite, gestures are taken up again which have already been used in initiation, it is first of all because these gestures point to the future. And it is equally because these gestures in combination express the manifold diversity of christian experience, a diversity intentionally recapitulated shortly after the baptismal rite proper.

These are therefore two reasons allowing understanding of the postbaptismal ceremonial to the extent that it repeats the prebaptismal symbolism. What follows the rite of water is also what has preceded it, that is, a hope and a messianic abundance of gifts.

But to these two themes must be added a third reason. The perception of the ancient liturgies, in the East as well as in the West, was to signify after the baptismal action that the baptised were identified with Christ and therefore bearers like him and in him of the Spirit. In other words the intention was to centre the trinitarian and ecclesial faith in which baptism is celebrated on the Spirit who dwells in Christ baptising.

To be baptised is therefore to be christened, christed.

On what does such an affirmation rest? In fact it is not obvious. One might think in effect that after the rite of water given in the name of the Father, the Son and the Holy Spirit it would be rather the presence of the Spirit we should want to stress. For to live as a baptised person is to live in the Spirit. Further, the two fundamental purposes I have just indicated, the desire to unfold the diversity of christian experience, and that of emphasising its eschatological bearing, must of their own accord meet in the 'spirit' sense of the baptismal life. The Spirit with the seven gifts, which is to say a manifold profusion, is equally the Spirit who has us await the end of time and the universal coming of the Kingdom. I add that for numerous christians what takes place after baptism is quite normally linked to the sacrament, something of an enigma, but basically referring to the Spirit, and which in the West is called Confirmation.

However, in spite of these indications I hold that the postbaptismal rites are in the first place centred on Christ. And if they refer to the Spirit, it is in the name of Christ as the Risen Son invoking his own Spirit.

What shows this is first of all the importance placed, in the West first and then in the East, on the anointing with oil performed on the newly-baptised. Now this rite signifies expressly the name of Christ, since that name means Anointed of God.[1] A person just baptised is therefore led to discover the personal saving mystery of Jesus Christ and to enter into his condition so as to share in his mission.

But, you will say, in the East the liturgies did not at first lay the same stress on the postbaptismal anointing as has been the case in the West. Agreed. Yet with other ritual gestures, notably the laying on of the hand, it is the same christological feature which is brought out.[2] And when the eastern liturgies make use of anointing it can be, it is true, with a bare formula such as the byzantine: "seal of the gift of the Holy Spirit", but it can also be characterising the oil, as the Syrians do, as "the good odour of Christ God" or, as the Armenians say, that it is "poured out in the name of Christ".

Obviously it is not a matter of isolating Christ from the Spirit. But rather of making the vital logic of initiation apparent. After the water of baptism it is under the sign of Christ the anointed of God that baptismal life is perceived and presented. The developing eschatology is his. The Spirit entering in is his. Just as Pentecost extends Easter and actively

1. In the West, several texts of the 3rd century, diverse in origin, are very plain. Tertullian: "On coming out of the bath of salvation a holy unction is poured on us . . . our name of 'Christ' (christian) comes from this oil whose unction also gives its name to the Lord" (De Baptismo, 7); Cyprian: "The newly baptised must receive the anointing: the oil he receives makes him the anointed of the Lord, possessing in himself the grace of Christ" (Letter 70,2); Hippolytus: "He shall be signed by the priest with the oil of thanksgiving with these words: 'I sign you with the holy oil in the name of Jesus Christ' " (Trad. Apost. 21). In the East, the anointing with oil has less clearly this 'christic' sense which quickly became obscured. It is found however, for example, in the syrian liturgy which presented the oil as "the good odour of Christ God".

2. See for example the postbaptismal prayer in the ancient chaldean ritual in I.-H. Dalmais, op.cit., p. 80–81. Baptismal eschatology for example is presented as a return to Christ.

makes remembrance of it, so the postbaptismal rites demonstrate the christic bearing of initiation.[1]

The forms of postbaptismal ritual

How to know then which symbolic rites are the most suited to developing this significance, rather takes second place. The rites of the white garment or the candle can both easily be linked to the Son of God, new transfiguring man. But these rites, which are late, are not the most fundamental. Equally, the second category of postbaptismal actions, the series directed towards the approaching eucharist, also usually takes on a christological sense. But it developed notably late, since the recent reforms in the West, and in any case would not suffice to express, as a close to the baptismal liturgy, all the significance of the mystery accomplished. This is why liturgical tradition, eastern and western, has especially valued a third group of actions, the most ancient and the most immediately biblical.

These actions are three in number: the anointing with oil, the laying on of hands or hand, the sign of the cross. They are three gestures performed on the body of the baptised. All three have already been employed during the initiation. Here they are re-enacted with the sense of eschatological and christological fulness, as the accompanying formula indicates. Whatever may be the complexities of liturgical history concerning them, one fact at least is plain: the various traditions appear to have originally preferred one or the other,[2] but very soon, from the beginning of the 4th century, there came to be formulated in the Churches as a whole,[3] by mutual borrowing or by development of the rites, a whole ritual comprising all three. And it is in regard to this group that the two other series of rites of which I have been speaking can be positioned.

Initiation after baptism

What meaning should be given to the combination anointing, imposition of hands and the sign of the cross?

The best thing is not to detail each of these gestures, attributing to

1. This 'christological concern' in initiation liturgy repeats in some sort that already found at work before the rite of water in the byzantine, syrian and coptic rituals, inviting the catechumens to choose Christ after having renounced Satan, anti-Christ. Yet another example of the continuity of ritual in one and another part of the rite of baptism.

2. For example: the anointing with oil is particularly western, whereas the ancient East did not know it and adopted at first the imposition of hands or the sign of the cross for the postbaptismal rite.

3. With exceptions. For example the non-catholic Chaldeans do not have the anointing.

each its own significance. They are three taken together expressing the three senses which christian initiation finds in the rite of water: the presence of Christ and the christic vocation of the christian, the diversity of gifts in baptismal life, the eschatological orientation, conclusive and eucharistic, of christian existence.

We can, it is true, distinguish these central lines of meaning. Provided we do not separate them.

Then it becomes possible to insist on the 'christening' to which baptism calls and makes possible. In this perspective, to sign the newly baptised with oil is another way of signifying that they have encountered Christ in his paschal mystery. What St Paul affirms of baptism in Romans 6 the liturgy manifests by making use of oil after water and consecrating the oil, in the same way as the water is blessed.[1] Or again, the 'christening' can lead on to announcing Christ's identity in his threefold office: "As Christ was anointed Priest, Prophet and King, so may you live always as a member of his body".

In the same way we can bring out the presence of the Spirit in the newly-baptised and emphasis their 'spiritualisation'. The prayer accompanying the solemn imposition of hands on the newly-baptised in the Roman ritual appears moreover as an 'epiclesis', that is an invocation of the Spirit, acting as a baptismal consecration brought about by the action of baptism.[2] Decidedly given to making explicit the presence of the Spirit, the western liturgy enumerates from the text of Isaiah 11 the seven gifts of the Spirit. Then, returning to byzantine soberness it invites the baptised to receive the 'seal' of the Spirit which is given them.[3]

Modulations of the symbolic

A second way of understanding the significance of the postbaptismal

1. We speak of 'blessing' baptismal water but 'consecrating' oil of chrism. This consecration, performed by the bishop, is still however a blessing. Formerly in the Roman liturgy the blessing of water involved pouring into it a little consecrated oil. This symbol appeared a little too forced and was not retained. It at least signified the close link between the significance of the oil and that of the water in christian initiation.
2. The term 'epiclesis' is ordinarily used for the eucharistic liturgy. It will be noticed that the western liturgy emphasises this aspect more than the eastern liturgies do, whereas it is usually the reverse in the eucharistic liturgical traditions.
3. This formula used for the sacrament of confirmation in the new 1978 ritual replaces the earlier form: "I seal you with the sign of the cross and I confirm you with the chrism of salvation. . .". It is a borrowing from the byzantine ritual and, as is traditional in this ordo, does not insist on the role of the minister. So much so that today western people are baptised after the usual manner in the West ("I baptise you . . .") and confirmed in the manner of the East which emphasises God's gift ("Be sealed with the gift of the Holy Spirit").

moment in initiation is to allow oneself to be guided by the original note each of the three main rites contributes to the whole when taken together. It being understood, I repeat, that it is not intended by this to separate them but rather in order the better to perceive how they accord.

Viewed in this perspective the accents are fairly clear. The anointing is the symbol of Christ the Messiah, his lordship and his three-fold office in the world. The imposition of hands is a gesture of deliverance which repeats that already accomplished and which in consequence recognises the danger beyond baptism of infidelity and the realisation of weakness which accompany the christian life. Finally, the sign of the cross is the mark of Christ in his passover of suffering, death and resurrection. And it is also as the gesture suggests a spiritual sign, a seal impressed on christians by the presence of Christ and his manifold Spirit.

What sacrament is there between baptism and the eucharist?

There is a third way of underlining the meaning of initiation in its postbaptismal phase. It is to recognise that something essential occurs at this point. Certainly what happens after the rite of water, develops and extends the meaning of that rite and depends on it. Further, what is celebrated after baptism, is directed towards what is to come, the eucharist particularly, and anticipates the future. Consequently the postbaptismal liturgy has not the same importance as the key actions, baptism and the eucharist. And yet this liturgy and its significance for christian initiation are not, I find, a simple transition. There are between baptism and the eucharist more than one intermediary period. Something constitutive is at work here.

This is what western theology means by declaring that confirmation is a sacrament. This affirmation has in the course of history not gone unchallenged. Even in the West it developed gradually. And in practice it was in the 12th century, when the sevenfold sacramentary was instituted, that confirmation was plainly given official inclusion among the sacraments. The Churches of the East, less given to systematisation than those of the West, rallied without much difficulty to this principle.[1] But the Lutheran Reform for its part refused this concept, esteeming it to be without sufficient biblical foundation to support it and that to interpret confirmation in sacramental terms was tantamount to minimising the sacrament of baptism.[2] The Reformers admitted however the

1. See especially the text of the Council of Florence in 1439.
2. cf. Lukes Vischer, *La confirmation au cours des siècles*, **Delachaux-Niestlé**, 1959.

possibility of a rite of blessing for the baptised before they made their first communion.

There is not the possibility here of furthering this debate. I shall content myself with two comments.

The first is that the qualification of sacrament given by the Catholic Church and the Churches of the East to confirmation does not mean that the initiation accomplished between baptism and the eucharist has the same formative nature as those two sacraments. For the Council of Trent it is plain, for example, that the sacraments are not all on the same level.[1]

Next, a second comment seems to me called for regarding the significance of sacramentality in initiation. It can certainly be spoken of in several ways: from the biblical standpoint, the point of view of the effects the rites have on us, the point of view of the original commitment of God and the Church in these actions. In the perspective which I adopt in this book, that of christian initiation, I would rather emphasise what there is of sacramental at one point in initiation where the continuous values being gradually discovered combine into one signal innovation. It is this which makes possible God's special intervention, that is to say at once recapitulating and innovating. It is this which constitutes for the initiates a recognisable stage in attaining christian experience. From this standpoint, to say what occurs after baptism and before communion has a sacramental bearing which is not without significance.

Baptised in the Spirit of Christ

What then is this new thing which enters after the rite of water and can be seen as something of the sacramental order in postbaptismal initiation?

This innovation is not to be found on the side of the rites. At any rate not the three main rites of anointing, laying on of hands and the sign of the cross.[2] At most it could be accepted that these three actions are here combined and inter-related. But this does not seem to give sufficient ground for the new thing we are looking for.

If then we turn to look at what is signified, the results of our inquiry are no more conclusive. These significances I have already said are three in kind: the diversity of baptismal life, the awareness of the future which is found in the baptised, the union with Christ and the Spirit of Christ, characteristic of christians. But these significances are not properly speaking new. Even though re-expressed and redeployed

1. 7th Session, can. 2.
2. Although the rite of water introduces something new into the order of symbols, as will the eucharistic action.

in terms of the rite of baptism, they do not constitute something original.

Well then? So, we have to state that the sacramentality of christian initiation in its postbaptismal phase flows from the sacramentality of baptism. It continues and enlarges on it but is not one with it. Consequently, to cut the matter short, what in the West we call confirmation is a sacrament only as dependent on the fundamental sacrament of baptism, as a remembrance of it and to reactivate it.

However, it is possible to be a little more precise by taking into account a liturgical factor to which I have already made allusion, that of epiclesis. Here there certainly is something new liturgically speaking in regard to the preceding sacramental action. In the eucharistic liturgy this is plain. Yet it is something new which expands or repeats, without properly speaking adding anything original. It is a matter of manifesting the intervention of the Spirit in the mystery of Christ which is being celebrated by expressing it as such, so that this mystery can be fully present.

I would say therefore that the postbaptismal innovation, giving rise to a sacrament, according to catholic and eastern christianity, is that the baptismal rite is to be seen and recognised as an act of the Spirit. For us humans there is need for two ritual moments in order to take in what from God's point of view is single. We are baptised in the Spirit because baptised in the name of Christ and the trinitarian act. But we need an epiclesis, an invocation of the Spirit, for us to realise what is accomplished in this baptismal action. It being understood that the Spirit of baptism is the Spirit of Christ, and that the liturgies experience the need to manifest the personal presence of Christ before emphasising that of the Spirit.

Remembrance in the Spirit

Baptism and postbaptismal initiation therefore form a single sacramental reality. The baptismal epiclesis follows on the consecration of the baptised just as the eucharistic epiclesis extends the consecration of the bread and wine, and formulates spiritually the dispositions of the assembled faithful.[1]

This theology of baptismal epiclesis can be aligned with what the ancients said in aligning confirmation with Pentecost and baptism with Easter. Pentecost is not properly speaking a paschal epiclesis, for the gift of the Spirit is not called down by the faithful. But it extends

---

1. The eucharistic epiclesis is directed towards the offertory: Christ offers himself to God in the Spirit and the christians present themselves in a spiritual offering joined to that of Jesus. The baptismal epiclesis too is animated by a like tendency: but the offering of the baptised is made in the eucharistic action, it does not yet take place in confirmation.

Easter and expresses its spiritual content.

From a more contemporary viewpoint I should like rather to link this theme of epiclesis in initiation to that of baptismal remembrance which I underlined at the beginning of this book. The epiclesis to the Holy Spirit extends in christian initiation the anamnesis constituted by the rite of water performed in the name of the Father, the Son and the Holy Spirit according to the command of Christ. It would certainly be an abuse of the word to say that it is a remembrance of what has just been done. Unless there were, as in the case in the East, a considerable lapse of time between the baptismal celebration and that of confirmation. But whichever way you look at it, in the East as in the West, the epiclesis repeats the anamnesis, takes it up again.

Initiation at the postbaptismal moment has therefore for aim to show just what is this baptismal remembrance which the act of baptism constitutes in us. We are baptised in the remembrance of the Risen Christ and so as to be able to make remembrance of him. But this remembering is not simply a human psychological faculty. It is a remembrance given by God, received by him. A faith-memory. That is, the actions which follow on the rite of water tell us this specifically, a remembrance in the Spirit. The baptismal anamnesis cannot exist unless it is also epiclesis.

You who have been baptised in Christ and confirmed in his Spirit, you can therefore confess, not only with St Paul that the Spirit prays in you, but equally that it is in you he makes remembrance of Christ and his Gospel, by virtue of the baptism which you have received.

*　　*　　*

Summary

What should be retained from these considerations on postbaptismal initiation?

— First of all that it is not superfluous. The baptismal rite does not centre in itself the whole meaning of the act of baptism. It calls for a *continuation.*

— It is evocative to note what the rituals put forward to extend the rite of water: eschatological and eucharistic *hope,* the *multiplicity* of gifts and aspects in the christian life, the deep relationship the baptised have with *Christ and his Spirit.*

— If we think of baptism as forming an active remembrance in those who receive it, plainly — and postbaptismal initiation undertakes to show this — that remembrance is exercised in the *Spirit.*

— There are differences of interpretation and practice between *West and East* concerning the initiation following on baptism and leading to the eucharist. But what I have brought out in the preceding pages constitutes a 'given' common to the different traditions. Allowing that the Lutheran and protestant Reform constituted a kind of warning against inflation of the action and against an inappropriate extension of the sacramental order.

11

To be christian
is to discover
at the end of initiation
the eucharist and
the paradox of the Church

Two unresolved problems

You have been baptised in Christ. You have put on Christ and received his Spirit so as to make remembrance of Easter in the world which God creates and calls to conversion. You have been initiated.

What else is there to do but live as a christian?

That means making remembrance of Christ in daily life and in Church life. Celebrating his presence and accompanying the action of his Spirit amid the hazards of the world and in the solidarities of the Church. Giving thanks to God all your days and celebrating his Kingdom in the sacraments.

And yet, what we have just gone over on the subject of christian initiation, is that sufficient to allow of living such a programme, or rather a vocation such as this?

In fact, initiating christians, through the prebaptismal stages, baptism, and the rites following, calls for two specific distinctions which today do not follow of themselves. First, on the subject of the postbaptismal moment. I have given its sense and bearing. But in western history there has been felt the need to give this moment a little more significance, especially by underlining the ecclesial aspect of christian life. Next, on the subject of the eucharist. For the eucharist is not solely the goal of initiation, that to which it is leading. It is an integral part of it. And that too needs to be made plain today.

Confirmation in the West

After the rite of water, the epiclesis invokes the Spirit on the baptised so that they may await the coming of the Kingdom in constancy and fidelity, so that they can know how to put to use the manifold aspect of the gifts which have been made known to them, so as to be christened at last and therefore able to live by the Spirit.

All this is no problem in the East. But it raises problems in the West. Why? Perhaps because we do not always know how to live in the Spirit. Especially because the course of history has meant that baptism became separated from one part of the postbaptismal initiation and was reconstituted in two celebrations distinct in time. We would have known only one sacramental moment in two movements as in the East, ritually and spiritually distinct but not isolated one from the other. We find ourselves in fact with two sacraments, distinct and the most often separate.

How did this separation come about? How is it that most of the postbaptismal rites, and especially the three having sacramental value, have been formulated apart? How are we to understand the fact that the conclusion to baptism is normally celebrated in the West several years after the rite of baptism, when it is its immediate continuation, and in the East follows on without a pause?

We could think of pastoral arguments and say that the instructional value of the stages before baptism is found again after the rite of baptism. In the same way as, from the earliest times in the Church, christianity constructed a way of initiation leading to baptism, so to pass from baptism to the eucharist it proposes an intermediary stage, called Confirmation in the West. But this first interpretation of the matter proves insufficient. Firstly because it is not valid for the East. Therefore it must be explained why eastern christians have not felt the need to dissociate the last part of the baptismal ceremony from the rite of water, when this was thought necessary in the West. Next because history furnishes a most interesting motivation for the western practice and allows of giving precise content to the stage of initiation which follows on baptism.

This motivation is as follows: the West was intent on signalising the place, role, and symbolism of the bishop in christian initiation much more strongly than is the case in the East. Or again, the Churches of the West have not wanted the part played by the bishop in christian initiation to become blurred, whereas the East adapted to the situation brought about by the expansion of the Church.

Mystagogia of the Church

To understand the difference of attitude we must begin by making explicit the reference to the bishop in christian initiation. It appears today after the baptismal rite in the East as well as in the West. But as is usually the case with initiation, an emphasis such as this coming in at this point is not something entirely new. At least in the West, and for adult initiation. You will remember the Election which the Roman ritual provides for adults going on to baptism. It is the bishop or his personal delegate who calls them individually to the sacraments of initiation when Lent begins.[1] However, this use is not maintained for infant baptism nor for that of children of school age. So that in fact the reference to the bishop and to what he represents is only to be found after the rite of baptism, in the West as in the East.[2]

It is, besides, an indication rather than an emphasis in most of the liturgical traditions: the oil of the anointing has been previously consecrated by the bishop and even in many eastern Churches by the patriarch.

Why this feature? It should be understood according to the logic of postbaptism which I have indicated above. To make a reference to the bishop at this point in the initiation does not mean that those initiated have waited until they were baptised, before discovering what the Church is and what significance the episcopal ministry has for her. But there is a time for everything. It is in fact after the rite of water that the need is felt to make explicit what has already been implied in initiation by an epiclesis following immediately, or again by a sacramental mystagogia. From this point of view there is a certain parallelism between the sense of the Holy Spirit made present then, and the sense of the Church which at this moment takes on greater exactness. In the same way as after the baptism an epiclesis invokes the presence of the Spirit already at work in the baptismal action, so the newly-baptised are 'christened' by realising that they are members of a local Church presided over by a bishop. On this point, western and eastern christians see the matter alike.

But this does not explain why the West wanted to emphasise further the link between initiation and the bishop's ministry. For this is the point. The reference to the bishop, made somewhat cautiously by the postbaptismal anointing, has not been judged sufficient in the West.

Baptism completed in presence of the bishop

It is at this point that history must be heard. In fact it is not that the West with an inflationist 'episcopalism' has added to the christian initiation of early times. But it has wished not to lose a symbolic element which the East has judged not indispensable, given the evolution of the Church.

1. In adult initiation, the bishop is, besides, expressly involved right at the start, for this initiation expressly depends on him. Cf. the general introduction to the Roman ritual for baptism (General Introduction 1.12) and the introduction to Christian Initiation of Adults (1.18). See also in the new Code of the Church canon 817.

2. From the 3rd to the 4th centuries the rite of water was performed by deacons, and afterwards the newly-baptised, on going into the 'cathedral', were anointed by the bishop who imposed hands on them.

In effect, when baptisms were no longer celebrated in the presence of
the bishop, which quickly became the normal procedure, it was established in the eastern Churches that the priest would celebrate as minister
of the whole initiation ceremony and that sufficient reference to the
bishop was made by the use of the chrism consecrated by him, and of
course by the presbyteral ministry. The West reacted otherwise. It was
decided that the bishop should continue to complete the initiation in
person. It was enough to wait for him to be in the area, and this in
practice gave a double ending to baptism. The priest who had presided
at the baptism would administer an anointing to the newly-baptised,
would give them the white garment and the candle. And later on the
bishop would impose hands and sign the new member of the Church
with the cross. Would he give another anointing? Custom varied on
this point. We have the impression that in the 4th to the 5th centuries
such a practice would seem strange: there is only a single anointing.[1]
But elsewhere it is to be met with, and finally determined the usage
which became current in the West.

Why this repetition of the anointing? For want of any exact docu-
mentation, a probable reason can be indicated. In the 4th century, for
Jerome or Ambrose, the actions performed by the bishop, at that time
the laying on of hands and the sign of the cross, are referred to the Holy
Spirit. It could be that this reference brought in a rite of anointing to
the extent that it is a biblical and liturgical manner of signifying the
Spirit. Thus this triple ritual 'complex' was formed of the imposition of
hands, the anointing and the sign of the cross with which the sacrament
of confirmation is celebrated today in the West.

The initiation process

As can be seen, the distinction between the two conclusions to the
baptism ceremony is not a strict separation. The anointing is doubled
and its repetition brings in again the continuity of the two baptismal
moments. At the same time, there is a difference between these two
moments, signalled by the presence of the bishop. The idea of this
arrangement is that one is not fully initiated by baptism, 'complete' as
they said in the ancient Church, without being in connection with the
bishop and what he represents in the local Church. All this is necessary,
in order to receive the Holy Spirit to the full extent.[2]

1. This is attested in the 4th century by Jerome, in the 5th by Pope
Innocent and the Council of Orange.
2. This is what Pope Cornelius said in the middle of the 3rd century about
someone who had been baptised but had not received the concluding rites:
"He has not received the other things which must be received according to
the rule of the Church and he has not received the sign of the cross made
by the bishop. Not having received all of that, how will he have received
the Holy Spirit?"

There still remains obviously a certain impression of doubling, given the two postbaptismal anointings. It can be understood in the sense that if, by hypothesis, baptism and confirmation were celebrated in the same ceremony[1] the first anointing would be suppressed and only the anointing of confirmation remain. But I should like to emphasise that historically it is the second anointing, that performed by the bishop, which repeats the first. And not the reverse. In other words, in the celebration of baptism the first anointing is not in any sense optional or superfluous. It has its own sense and is not merely an anticipation of the anointing of confirmation.[2] In fact, the formulas and rites have sought to make clear that the two anointings are not strictly equivalent. The first is accompanied by a phrase emphasising the 'christening' of the newly-baptised, while the second stresses only the gift of the Spirit. Next, the Roman ritual provides that priests perform the anointing on the head whereas bishops place the oil on the forehead.[3]

These two differences are not mere subtlety. They are enlightening, to my mind, in view of initiation. As I have said, christian initiation proceeds as a continuity. In this sense, the repetition of the anointing is only one particularly noticeable case of a practice running all through the initiation process. In fact, confirmation adds to baptism no radically new effect: it extends it, prolongs it in epiclesis on the one hand, by ecclesial realism on the other, but it is not properly speaking either a sacrament of the Spirit, as though the Spirit had not been already imparted to the baptised, nor a sacrament of the Church as though experience of the Church had not already, before the rite of water even, been impressed on the life of the new christians. Confirmation is not inaugural; it furthers the possibilities and consequences of baptism. It 'confirms' baptism.

1. This is what the ritual for adults provides. Experience shows that this way of proceeding is not necessarily desirable pastorally and that even for adults it is ordinarily an advantage not to celebrate confirmation at the same time as baptism. It will be noticed in any case that a priest who administered baptism to an adult can also in principle administer confirmation. This arrangement returns to the consideration that the presence of the bishop is not required in initiation. Or else that the minister of baptism is in a position to symbolise what traditionally in the West is signified by the minister of confirmation. Or in any case is not inserted into the line of western tradition. The first seems preferable to me. Except for one thing: for adults called up to baptism by the bishop, the episcopal presence has already been made significant.

2. I may be allowed to emphasise this point in consideration of certain pastoral hesitations at the present time.

3. Letters of Pope Innocent I, at the beginning of the 5th century.

The significance of confirmation in initiation

We can see therefore how baptismal initiation takes on greater depth under the sign of confirmation.

I find three significant elements, of which the first two are common to the East and to the West.

First of all the aspect of *epiclesis* or mystagogia. It is after the event that we realise what we have received. It is by being confirmed that we can best embrace the baptism which has entered our lives. Better, it is in line with the first anointing that in the West the second is understood. For the Spirit symbolism of the second anointing presupposes that the newly-baptised are united to Christ, bearers of his christic condition, already Spirit-filled.

Next, confirmation is presented as a *structural* or connecting sacrament. It draws together not only the rites — anointing, imposition of hands, sign of the cross — but also their meanings. These are two. On the one hand, the presence of the Spirit; on the other the reference to the bishop. To be confirmed is to be qualified by God himself to live a baptismal life, able to 'keep in hand' these two constituent realities. For to be christian is to live at once in the Spirit and in the Church.

It appears to me that it is here we find the most fundamental sense of confirmation in the West.[1] It is the one logically demanded by the liturgy and by history. It is equally the one which avoids a certain number of platitudinous notions such as the one which sees confirmation as an 'extra', an accretion in regard to baptism. That there is added depth is certain. But in what sense, in what way? The sacrament of confirmation marks out a route. One is confirmed in baptism when in a position to live christianity at the same time and with the same desire both as freedom in the Spirit and as institutional allegiance, a spirituality imprisoned in no law and an historic reality which makes for solidarity with other christians, their past, their hopes and difficulties, their mission, in fine.[2]

Lastly, third point, confirmation in the West imparts time to the programme of christian initiation, the principle of stages. In other words, after baptism it continues with the prebaptismal instruction: it

1. For a fuller treatment may I refer the reader to: *L'avenir de la confirmation*, pp. 152–54, Le Chalêt, 1972; *Confirmation, sacrement pour aujourd'hui* (in conjunction with M. Michel and G. Pinckers), Le Chalêt, 1982, p. 11–44).
2. This meeting of the spiritual and the institutional in the christian life implies that in the liturgy of confirmation there is an understanding of ordained ministry and most precisely that of the bishop. In other words, confirmation 'seals' a deepening sacramentality. To be confirmed is to realise that the minister is not the whole of the Church but that he expresses her mission as structural. Confirmation and the bishop are therefore equivalent signs.

takes time to become a christian. It is somewhat strange to record that the West has felt such a need when the East has not experienced it. I would tend to think that, as things are, confirmation presents a kind of 'sacrament of the West'. For in its western form it takes note of difficulties particularly strong in the West. We find it hard to live in the Spirit, we find it hard to live in the Church; with our love of organisation and our continual dissatisfaction regarding institutions, we are after all too little prepared to understand the mysterious unity between life in the Spirit and life in the Church.

The eucharist initiates

Initiation is not however complete yet. For baptism, even though confirmed, looks to the eucharist, where communion in the Spirit can be experienced and nourished by ecclesial communion in the Church.

We ordinarily maintain that first communion is one of the sacraments of initiation, but we are not necessarily clear on the subject. So let us attempt to define what this means.

In the first place I would say that it implies a certain way of presenting and speaking of *baptism.* A person is not baptised with no reference to the eucharist, with no orientation to that act which assembles and gives life to the Church of the baptised. But this is often passed over in silence today. Whether in preparing for baptism, where we do not want to give the impression of falling into legalism over the Sunday observance; or, equally in adult initiation, as for children of school age: the course is so centred on baptism that we almost forget to speak about communion.

Inversely, it should be observed that the eucharist initiates on condition that *other rites* have been celebrated before it and other fundamental discoveries already made. Initiation does not begin with the eucharist, according to the christian tradition.

This merits consideration today when we find sometimes doubts on this point. Non-baptised people, children or adults, are invited to the eucharist. Some even live out their whole initiation under the sign of the eucharist having given their allegiance to a massing community. Apart from juridical problems presented by this situation, and which are not the most important, it appears to me that this poses a pastoral and theological question. On the one hand the eucharist does not in effect afford in the one rite, as does baptism, the possibility of an individual profession of faith. Baptism reminds us in effect that belonging to the Church does not operate by general agreement, spontaneous aggregation, presumed faith. For she receives newcomers, satisfied to go on with her usual celebrations. She does not disturb herself, does not suit herself to the ways of the new christians.

Eucharist and confirmation

Altogether therefore the eucharist has initiatory value when it man-tains a two-way connection with baptism: baptism is oriented to the eucharist, the eucharist makes remembrance of baptism.

Can the same argument be made for confirmation? Is there the same connection between the eucharist and confirmation as between the eucharist and baptism?

In theory, yes. For, still in theory, the eucharist comes after confir-mation and presupposes therefore what confirmation performs in regard to initiation. It being understood again here that confirmation should as far as possible manifest in its catechesis and its celebration that it is under the same heading as the eucharist. It being accepted likewise that the eucharist makes operational a confirmed faith marked by a sense of the Spirit and a sense of the Church.

But in practice, at least in the West, it is not like that. For as things are, the new christians communicate before being confirmed, most often. Which is understandable, given the tendency to set back in time the moment of confirmation, whether to allow the bishop to be present, whether, especially today, to let the baptised mature in their baptismal faith. In other words, in the West, especially since 'early' communion for children was desired by Pius X, baptism has as its first consequence, full participation in the eucharist, and it is not until later that it is extended into confirmation. It is likewise this custom which is the most frequent in France for adult initiation.

This state of things is habitually regarded as suspect by historians, as by certain theologians. They consider it does not respect the logic of christian initiation. To hear them, the eastern custom would be more logical and more simple. It would be better to link confirmation to the celebration of baptism, at the risk of giving up the episcopal sign dear to the western tradition. Furthermore, they add that this sign should not be made into a fetish and it can have its equivalents for experiencing initiation.

Initiation is not purely linear

This course of argument does not seem to me very convincing, how-ever much truth there is in it.

Firstly, it appears to me a very suggestive thought that we westerners have the form of confirmation which suits what we are. For we have difficulty in actually living in ecclesial unity, and at the same time it is hard for us to realise the presence of the Spirit in the world and in the Church. These two handicaps are not found to the same degree in the christians of the East, less legalistic and less concerned about institutions than we are, more directly spiritual than we appear to be.

The problem is therefore as follows: would it be better to restore to initiation its traditional order and forgo the pastoral advantages of late confirmation? or would it be better to modify the normal sequence of initiation, given what confirmation received with psychological and spiritual maturity can do for us today in the West?

For my part I would answer the problem with the second suggestion. To maintain confirmation under its western form is of more interest than to reintegrate it with the eucharist in the initiation process. That is an innovation certainly. But liturgical history is there precisely to emphasise that in this matter the place and significance of confirmation are not particularly static.

There ensues a second challenge to the western practice — and particularly the French — today. If confirmation is celebrated after first communion, sometimes aften even a considerable period of eucharistic life, can it not be said that it confirms not only baptism but equally that first eucharistic experience? I think so. But on two conditions.

The first is that this initial phase of eucharistic life should be considered as in reality forming part of initiation, which means that it must be accompanied by the Church.

The second condition, more theological, is that the course of initiation should not be thought of as purely linear. If confirmation comes after first communion, that means that the connection between baptism and confirmation and the connection between baptism and the eucharist are at two different levels. Or again that baptism is extended in two complementary but distinct fashions, into eucharist and into confirmation. The traditional usage consists in imparting the one after the other. The present practice has returned to imparting the one in function of the other. Confirmation is neither more important, nor superior, to first communion. It is other. And baptism calls for the one and the other.

Innovation by the eucharist

I should like to introduce one last element regarding the initiatory value borne by the eucharist, by pointing out two elements in the eucharist characteristic of the whole initiation process: continuity and innovation.

The continuity between the eucharist and the preceding ceremonies is obvious. In connection with baptism, first of all. The eucharist extends the meanings of baptism: the fundamental gift of the future which is the Kingdom, the presence of Christ and his Spirit, the paschal mystery, liberation from sin, participation in the Church, her unity and her mission. From the point of view of the rites, equally it takes up again certain gestures of the baptismal celebration which are also in some cases expressly directed to the eucharist: the general intercessions, recitation of the Lord's Prayer, final blessing of the people present.[1] With regard to confirmation it is the same, but perhaps less clearly. So some of the senses of confirmation are certainly taken up again in the eucharist, or anticipated by it if it is celebrated before confirmation: the 'christological centring', the presence and invocation of the Spirit in epiclesis form, eschatological expectation, diversity of christian life, belonging to the Church. But the eucharistic rites scarcely resume those of confirmation or do not exactly anticipate them.[2] No anointing, no imposition of hands, in the eucharist. And the sign of the cross which is found there, for example in the final benediction, is in the first place baptismal.

No doubt these assertions should not be pushed too far. I shall merely interpret them by saying that continuity of the eucharist with baptism and confirmation is actual but not precisely the same in both bases. The eucharist is at least as closely linked with baptism as with confirmation. This tends to confirm that baptism extends into two sacramental rites, which do not constitute a linear series but form rather as it were two distinct and complementary continuations of it.

It is from this foundation of modulated continuity that springs the sacramental innovation of the eucharist.

On the level of meaning, the eucharist gives value to two factors which had so far not been proposed as such in the course of initiation. They are first the aspect of adoration and thanksgiving in the christian life: then the manifestation of the union of the baptised in the mystic Christ, through the symbols of food and drink. Finally there is the affirmation of the Church as the body of Christ turned towards the end of time. Three new dimensions of the christian life to be experienced by joining with Christ in his death, and daily facing our own.

On the level of the rites, the newness is equally symbolic. In the Mass it is not the water of baptism which signifies christian life and makes it a reality, nor the anointing, the imposition of hands, nor the sign of the cross so important in confirmation, but the bread and the wine which institute the nourishment of faith and ensure its festal song. Initiation therefore is going to the root of its corporeal aspect. The rites are no longer performed on the body of the initiate, they enter as festal food and drink. Likewise, in the Mass the Church is no longer only a community of baptismal reception and gospel resolve, no longer just a paradoxical gathering where the spiritual and the institutional meet, it

1. In addition the eucharistic prayer has a parallel in the blessing of the baptismal water.
2. Even though the eucharist can be presented as a confirmation in accordance with the ritual multiplicity typical of the postbaptismal phase of initiation.

is the body of every day, and of hope, of witness and of faithfulness, Jesus' self-giving in the Holy Spirit.

*   *   *

Summing up

Let us check off the points made about the conclusion to christian initiation:

— First of all, in the West postbaptismal initiation has doubled into *two distinct moments*. Some of these rites have remained linked to the baptism ceremony, the others have grouped at a distance and taken a name peculiar to the West, that of confirmation. Whereas the East has kept the unity of the postbaptismal initiation and given it the ancient name of anointing or seal.

— The western innovation is not without grounds. For the early Church spontaneously aimed at giving to christian initiation a *sign of ministry which was episcopal*. This sign does not double that other ministerial sign which is the intervention of the deacon or the priest in the liturgy of initiation. It completes this by enlarging it. The bishop indeed expresses ecclesial ministry under a broad or localised form of unity and with explicit reference to the apostolic tradition.

— The western attitude consists in giving value at the postbaptismal point of initiation to a significance not new but needing to be re-expressed characteristically at this point. It is *Church allegiance*.

This allegiance is thenceforward clearly determined. It is much more so here than at the moment when the new believers enter the Church or receive their baptism. It is in effect defined by reference to the bishop, that is by connection with what he represents.

What the bishop represents can no doubt be variously accented. But in one way or another what he signifies always returns to certain great fundamental aspects in the life of the Church and of christians: the unity of the local Church, its concrete form which is therefore institutional, the concern for evangelisation, the sense of tradition which makes remembrance of the past of faith so as the better to receive the present gift of God and prepare for the future.

— These things being so, they lead us to supply the three main significances of postbaptismal initiation. I have pointed out in the preceding chapter what were these essential significances: hope of the Kingdom, diversity of spiritual aspects or forms of baptismal life, christing and therefore the presence of the Spirit in the lives of the baptised. Now must be added this *other factor* which might have been held to be sufficiently indicated by the earlier points of initiation but which has to be renewed and re-expressed beyond baptism: Church allegiance. The Church in question is a Church recognised in the bishop and which the bishop recognises and confirms. Therefore a Church with local unity, wider than the small group to which each christian belongs. A Church visible and recognisable, refusing to allow itself to be enclosed in idealist dreams and projects. A Church of the Gospel, of tradition, and also bold in hope.

— In fact, the West does not limit itself to requiring significant additions to those traditionally proposed for the postbaptismal part of initiation. It requires especially that this significance should enter into the characteristic movement of postbaptismal initiation, that is that it should *have reference* to that form of epiclesis or invocation of the Spirit which finds a place at this point.

— In other words, according to the experience of the West, baptism does come to an end of itself and of its possibilities unless it is expressed *both* as life in the Spirit of Christ and as allegiance to the Church of that same Christ. At once freedom in the Spirit and fidelity to communion and allegiance.

— These two dimensions of baptismal life constitute a paradox which marks out a difficult route for christianity but one which is realistic and liberating. There is no doubt it needs time and experience to realise what this means. And it will be understood that in many cases today, out of habit, or prudence, or want of spiritual strength, people do not venture so far. But the line is open. The 'folly' of confirmation is that of a Church ceasing to oppose freedom and unity, spiritual freshness and institutional cohesion.

— Thus confirmation is found to be a *mark of the West*. It integrates into the sacramental order of initiation cares and aspirations which are ours. It is as though in the common framework of christian initiation Churches and people could legitimately evaluate what as they see it should be stressed locally, for the candidates, individuals always, to come to the unique christian faith.

— The eucharist is not to be underrated in this same context. It is not only what there is, once initiation is over; it finds a place *within initiation*, extending baptism in a different way from confirmation. It imparts to the programme of initiation three foundational experiences: personal and collective adoration in the form of thanksgiving, union with Christ and his Spirit under the sign of food and drink, understanding of the Church to be the body, as society and as mystery, of the Risen Christ.

— These eucharistic values in initiation can be misunderstood. They only really enter in if those instructing do not omit to make mention of the eucharist when there is question of baptism, and if the celebration of the eucharist makes remembrance of baptism. It is not for all that a matter of 'overloading' first communion. Nor of putting too much responsibility for initiation onto the eucharist alone as though initiation were entirely concentrated on it. Rather, we are asked to discover simply the *innovation* the eucharist provides with reference to baptism. And this innovation seems to me to be all the more recognisable by the fact that baptism is taking on meaning and importance in contemporary christian experience.

— The connection between the eucharist and confirmation can take many forms, given the variable position of the second with regard to the first, at least in the West. Here we have *a second western 'novelty'*.

— This second novelty is not so intentional as the first. It is rather a resultant, a matter of fact: in the West, many baptised take part in the eucharistic communion. But this fact gives pause. When it is the case it leads us to understand confirmation as confirming not only baptism *but also the initiation eucharist.*

— It remains then to define the practical relationships between the two sacramental celebrations, confirmation and the eucharist. I could wish for my part that the liturgy of confirmation were *not necessarily* followed by the eucharistic liturgy. Certainly, if the two are linked together there results a quite enlightening sequence. But there is the risk of seeing the eucharist 'overshadow' confirmation. As though the latter could not stand alone and give rise to an autonomous celebration significant of itself.

— In any case it does appear to me that the connection between confirmation and baptism is *not immediate*. It is by making a remembrance of baptism that confirmation and the eucharist initiate the baptised.

— It could therefore be said that confirmation intervenes as intermediary between baptism and the eucharist. But it must be held at the same time that the eucharist can also have a *direct relationship* with baptism and that in this case it is the eucharist which 'mediates' the connection between baptism and confirmation.

12

What is effected
by christian initiation?

To what is one initiated?

Now it is time to distinguish the main lines of meaning in christian initiation.

I should like to do so by a consideration of initiation as a whole. Certainly the various stages of the process and especially the three sacraments along its length can legitimately have an original bearing and particular accents. But, while allowing these obvious particularities, I should like to see what initiation produces as a whole. This standpoint is still not taken up enough today, it appears to me.

On the other hand, as I have done earlier, I shall look at initiation without reducing it to the sacraments structuring it.

Finally, it appears to me indispensable to introduce for analysis some simple distinctions. I shall seek first of all to indicate in their respective situations the subjects or parties which intervene in initiation. Then I shall order the results or contributions of the initiatory process.

It is God who initiates

Who intervenes in the initiation making a christian, and who allows it? Three actors are on stage, differently placed, but conducting the action together: God, the Church, the subject of the initiation.

It is important to begin by naming God. For we have the tendency today to define christian initiation from our standpoint, in connection with our needs or expectations, when it is in the first place and before all God's investment in humanity. It is God who initiates, he takes the initiative.

Besides, that is a fact given emphasis by initiation. Firstly by the role it assigns to the Word of the Bible, a real and efficacious presence of God in the world and among believers. In the judeo-christian faith, a start is always made with acceptance of the Word, given as strength and light. Equally, the divine initiative is emphasised by the role of the minister of the Church, deacon, priest or bishop, who is not only agent of the Church, but a sign of God's priority in the life of faith. Christian theology has often remarked that we do not baptise ourselves but have been baptised by another in the name of that Other, mysterious yet present, God himself. The formula can be extended: we do not initiate ourselves, we are initiated, we enter into an initiating tradition, we join in a remembrance, we are introduced into a movement of history begun long before our own lives. Lastly, God's gift is further signified by the prayer of petition and thanksgiving, which accompanies the candidates and those initiating them all along their journey together, and indicates clearly enough how both groups are dependent on a mystery and a Spirit not attributable to human experience or wisdom.

God's initiatory action a reality

Let us attempt to define God's action in the action of initiation.

I would say first of all that it is a reality. It is not to be reduced to a play upon words. It does not enter in simply as a manner of speaking. It must, indeed, be admitted that this causes difficulties today sometimes. In the West, many people believe in God but rest content more or less with faith in his existence. Which obviously scarcely respects the biblical and gospel testimony. Or else we believe in a God who acts, but in a global way, universal, supra-temporal. And we are a little shy of imagining an action of the Lord of the universe as concerned with one single human being, at a moment fixed by the human calendar. That seems suspect of naive anthropomorphism. Sometimes it even appears improper, in regard to the transcendent mystery of God.

And yet christian initiation does not yield on this point. It even claims to bear within its dynamic the means of overcoming these doubts and reservations. It holds that each of us is initiated individually — which is not to say in isolation — and that we are all named, called, and showered with blessings by a God who knows our most intimate and individual selves.

The whole thing is to understand clearly how God does really act for each of us. It would effectively be inept to picture to ourselves the active presence of God in too human a manner or as a vague outpouring over each creature. When we think of God it would appear obvious to go to the essential. This essential is called creation. And it is what is called the new creation: salvation. Understanding by this that these two actions are closely connected: saving people is another way for God of creating. Therefore to be initiated into gospel salvation, to the gift of the Kingdom, sets us in line with creation. To be baptised is to let God complete in us what he has begun.

But how is to be done? It is beyond us, certainly. We can at best understand a little of what happens, by thinking of God's action as always going from the universal to the particular. In this sense, when

God initiates us into the christian faith and the mystery of his Kingdom and his Son, he *applies to each* what he wants to *do for all*. He individualises in us his cosmic universal mystery. He gives us an active and a passive share in his plan of creation and re-creation.

God's action in regard to each of us is therefore no different from his all-embracing fundamental action in regard to the world. The one is not additional to the other. But the one makes the other a concrete reality. By initiating us into the christian faith God confirms what he has undertaken in the world by his Son and his Spirit.

Consequently, to believe in the action of God in the sacraments of initiation and more broadly still in the process as a whole, is not more difficult than to believe in his fundamental action in the universe. For us these two actions are different and consecutive. For God they are integrated into one unique will.

Initiation and God's universal love

We have another problem with us when we try to form some idea of the divine action within initiation. We ask ourselves whether such an action does not constitute a sort of privilege reserved to the few and whether it does not go counter to the universal love of God for all humankind.

Here again the important thing seems to me to ask the right question. And for this we have to rely on what is most universal in God's action. The offer of salvation, the suggestion that we might live in the Spirit and in the Kingdom, God makes these to everyone. And he makes them present by many means in history. Christian initiation is *only one of the ways* by which he brings to each one the universal invitation. This way is certainly incomparable. It goes to the depth of the Christ mystery. But it is not the only way for God to love and save the world.

What then does the fact of being initiated into the christian faith mean? It is a vocation, a call. It is not merely the opportunity for the candidates to take stock of what they are being given. It is a divine intervention properly called. What does it aim at? God desires to form in the world a people of witness, a community which is to be the body of his Son. Not to make a ghetto people. But so that what God wishes to do for and with them may be demonstrated before all humanity. The christian vocation is therefore at the service of our human vocation. The re-creating relationship which God seeks with each human being is antecedent to that which he wants with each christian. And that is the effective sign of the other.

To be initiated is therefore not to be got out of difficulties, to draw a 'lucky number'. It is to accept that one's life should be a witness so that humanity as a whole can as far as possible be re-created by God.

Initiation into God's commitment as Trinity

One last way of understanding God's action in christian initiation is to think of it as trinitarian. This follows necessarily, since any act of God is so.

This is a familiar standpoint.

We can first of all say that in very truth our initiation has essentially re-created us in God. This we express by speaking of a new birth, or again by saying that christian initiation has made human beings into sons and daughters of the living God, having with him a bond of knowledge and of love.

It appears to me all the same that we have to watch language to avoid giving the impression that God would not love us if we were not baptised. The gift of God and the faith it calls into being certainly constitute in us a filiation. But this christian vocation does not mean exclusiveness, as though non-christians too could not live in filial fashion with regard to God, however obscurely. If this were indeed the case I do not see how christianity could affirm that salvation in Jesus Christ is offered to all, and that non-christians who have not had a genuine possibility of believing in the Gospel are associated to Christ's paschal mystery, are therefore filiated.

We must therefore avoid saying without further qualification that *baptism makes a child of God*. It is better to assert that it is God's love for human beings which makes them sons and daughters of God in Jesus Christ and in his Spirit. Baptism and initiation as a whole are not, for all that, unnecessary. They are not reduced to giving explanations, as though the candidate was merely given the means of understanding a general vocation of which many were ignorant of the significance and bearing. I would say rather that the sacraments of faith make us a child of God in a specific fashion, by associating us with those for whom Christ is *historically* responsible. Initiation sanctifies by evangelising us.

From this viewpoint, to be initiated is therefore not only to be re-defined before God, re-created by him, but it is also to have part in Christ's pasch and in his gospel, and it is to be a bearer in one's life of the Spirit of Christ, Spirit of the Last Days and also inspiration of the Gospel. By being made christian and becoming what we are, we are not only taken up into God's life and the mystery of the Trinity, but equally, plunged into God's commitment in history, that commitment, again, having trinitarian form, since it expresses in human terms the being of God.

The Church initiates on God's initiative

It is therefore God who takes the primary initiative in Christian initiation. But his action is in association with that of the Church. The

K

Church in her turn, in her degree, initiates.

At present, this ecclesial aspect of initiation bulks large in our thinking and practice. We are well aware that the sacraments are not purely
personal or private acts. And we understand quite well that we do not
go to God, or rather that God does not come to us to make us christians,
without our entering the mystery of the Church. Even though God is
also working in the world and even though we also go to him through
our daily lives in the world.

Yet I do not know whether we sufficiently realise in our age the
Church's mission to initiate.

For example, we affirm following Augustine and tradition that a
person is baptised — and therefore in the wider sense initiated — 'in the
faith of the Church'. In other words, all candidates for initiation, infant
or adults, are plunged into a faith antecedent to and embracing their
own individual outlook. But, it appears to me, if the Church initiates,
it is not simply because she believes. It is because of her way of believing, which is reception of the gift of God. Basically the Church initiates
through her own faith because she bears within her the spring of all
faith, I mean the Word of God and also that Christ-mystery enshrined
in her as in a body.

A subtlety you will say. Between the faith of the Church and the
sources of that faith there is only a minor distinction. I agree. But this
divergence could well indicate that not all faith is necessarily in a
position to initiate. There are believers who indoctrinate or inoculate
others with their own troubles but who do not initiate. For initiation is
a founding work. Or again a source work. To be able to help in discovering the well-springs in others it is necessary to be oneself aware
of what it is to be reborn and humbly open to the divine gift.

It is doubtless, in this perspective, possible to bypass a difficulty
brought up here and there nowadays, regarding a certain ecclesial
'inflation' in understanding or in the practice of christian initiation.
Whether it is a question of baptism or of confirmation and the eucharist,
some consider too much emphasis is placed on the ecclesial dimension
of these sacraments. They say that baptism is not in the first place
belonging to the Church but first of all a gift of God, that confirmation
in not first and foremost taking up responsibility in church and secular
life but a Pentecost of the Spirit. They add that the eucharist is not
above all an assembly but acts primarily as adoration and thanksgiving.
These reactions are not without foundation. But they seem to me to
call less for restoring the balance between the christological and the
trinitarian in an initiation considered too ecclesial, than for a deepening
of what the Church of initiation means.

In fact, the Church is not in the first place a social body. She receives herself from God as the body of Christ and mystery of the Spirit. If she initiates, it is precisely by making appear in what she says, what she does, and what she is, the initiative of God for whom she exists.

To live as initiate, to be able to initiate

In practice the Church is not good at initiating unless she keeps alive within herself the sense of initiation.

This means that initiation is one of her essential functions. I do not intend to detail here the essential responsibilities of christian communities. Besides they can be looked at in several ways. But whatever the case, whatever the frame of reference, the main guidelines are always the same: gospel witness in the world, listening to the Word of God and prayer, working together and caring for unity, reception and training of new believers. What the Church does with and for newcomers is not, then, an additional secondary task. Rather, it seems to me that the major functions of the Church influence one another. In this sense, christian initiation doubtless results from what can be found in christian groups as a whole. It is marked by the stresses and strains of the time. But inversely it is in a position to influence other ecclesial actions. And this is the significance of the 'wave of catechumenism' (some more prudently say: a spirit of catechumenism) or baptismal renewal, currently spoken of in the Church of France today.

On the other hand when christian communities focus on their responsibilities in initiation they are led to rediscover many important features of their ecclesial vocation. Basically the programme of initiation gives a kind of *extended* formulation of what the Church is and this allows time to discover progressively the vital logic of the whole. The Church of initiation experiences herself as a welcoming community, a group where the Word of the Gospel is proclaimed, a present reality which calls, a space for liberation and confession of faith, a place where God expressly enters in, a communion in the Spirit, an organisation and at the same time an experience of the Spirit, a gathering where some members have a ministerial role, local solidarity and belonging to an international body, a duration where what has been begun demands to be confirmed, an assembly for adoration and thanksgiving, a community where there is remembrance and therefore hope.

Thus the Church does not know what she is except by doing what she is.

Are the initiates doing anything?

Let us come then to the third 'party' in initiation: this is the actual candidate, as a person and as a believer.

Concerning this presence of the candidate at the initiation, one problem runs through history and demands explanation today as yesterday. It bears on *the initiative of the person being initiated.* We wonder especially, when initiation begins such a short time after birth, just how active the boy or girl being presented to God and the Church is likely to be.

The question is certainly somewhat acute in what concerns infant baptism. But it is also valid for initiation for adults, for they are in fact invited to follow a course, enter on a catechesis and a ritual, only partly negotiable. Are they therefore passive?

Adults are given the desire
and the means of changing

I will begin with the second instance, as it is perhaps more straightforward and allows me to approach that of the newly-born more dispassionately.

What active part do adult candidates take in the process of their initiation? It is greater than is supposed. Not only because the programming of the course takes account of individuals and is personalised as far as possible, but also because experience shows that adult candidates experience a psychological and spiritual change which in no way condemns them to passivity. Some of the catechumens begin to dare to take a decision they had been deferring, undertake a demanding course of action, enter on effective ties of solidarity. Not all, certainly, are militants by nature. Besides, some, even before they began to discover the faith, had known what life would require of courage, imagination, and tenacity. For them then it is not certain that christian initiation much modifies commitments already undertaken. But in any event the catechumens say they enter into a freedom and light which change their way of seeing certain aspects of life.

What is interesting is to see how this change works. It is not willed. It appears rather to flow normally, freely, from faith in God. In other words, it is indeed a kind of passivity arising from confidence in God. But this passivity, which is welcoming a gift or bonus, has its *effects* in the order of responsibility and courage. The catechumens feel themselves called to believe in Christ, and the Gospel which they are discovering calls them to change their lives.

This experience continues also throughout initiation. A person is made a christian, but invited to become one. Initiation leads on to making remembrance of what one already is and to active correspondence with it. A person is baptised, confirmed, receives communion. But these verbal passivities open out onto activities in life. We do not baptise ourselves, but we try to live our baptism. We do not confirm ourselves. But confirmation received, reactivates baptismal life. We do not produce communion, we receive it. But in christian language it is an 'act' of all the people together.

Baptism of the newly-born

As for baptism of little children, here the position is obviously different. The newly-born can be admitted to baptism without their knowledge. It is not easy to see how they could take an active part.

A surprising fact surely. We understand certainly that existence is antecedent to us in a way. It is quite obvious that human life has been given to us without any activity on our part. But how is it that the rite of baptism, a 'second birth', should be as much arranged without our conscious free-will as is our first birth? Baptism does not appear to break out of the ordinary repetitive *round of events* weighing us down and conditioning our fate. And in the eastern Churches this situation includes more than baptism since the newly-born receive not only baptism but also chrism and communion.

It is not enough to justify these practices by comparing them to the conditioning to be found in all *education.* Precisely because education is never characterised by this alone: those being educated are never entirely passive. As for comparing christian initiation with what a new-born child's family does for its health or feeding, it can be seen that this is scarcely conclusive. For the gift of God is of another order.

It must therefore be admitted that the custom of baptising the newly-born constitutes a *paradox.* The Church does not want to wait before beginning initiation. And she does it by a sacramental rite in which God acts, the Church acts, but the child being initiated does not act. You will say then that the infant acts 'indirectly', by reason of solidarity with those presenting the child to the Church. But that seems circumstantial quibbling. And in any case it still remains that baptism comes in as an act of God, radically preceding any action by the baptised.

By acting in this way, christian tradition is not unaware of the question as I emphasised it earlier. But it disregards it. It makes light of the difficulty. It wants to begin the initiation of the newborn child by insisting that God comes first. Never mind that at some periods like ours such boldness seems somewhat incomprehensible and ought to give way to other practices less quick off the mark, as for example what today is called the welcoming, that is, initiation with a temporary interval before the baptismal rite itself.

Re-creation of free-will

Baptism of the newly-born is therefore baptism in a challenging form. It is a baptism not concerned about fine shades of meaning.

Once again, such a way of acting is neither always nor necessarily the most suited pastorally today. But, as it is, it faces us with a major point of christianity, that concerning our freedom before God. It sets us at the heart of this secular debate. It takes us straight to the fundamentals of christian spirituality. Instead of adopting a prudently advancing rhythm, initiation gives entrance without waiting into the family secrets of christianity. But it is plain that really to understand what is at stake there should be time and possibility or opportunity to experience christian life. Which is not given to everybody today.

What is the point, basically? It is a question of believing that God, by intervening before we can, does not undermine our free-will, but on the contrary re-creates it. God seems to ignore our liberty, but it is in order to liberate us. He takes the initiative so that we can become capable of taking up our life. He does not enter into competition with us. His action authorises ours. His presence does not prevent us from being present to ourselves.

If this is understood people cannot but be edified by such christian audacity. But if, for want of christian experience, it is seen as taking away our liberty, people will think of it as a serious misjudgment and that the Church must inquire into her practices.

What happens
to the newly-baptised?

It remains to ask ourselves what precisely the ceremony of baptism does for the newborn child receiving it. We tend sometimes to say merely that the newly-baptised is received into the Church. And obviously that is so. But is it enough? In order to go further, let us attempt rather to reformulate the question. Instead of trying to define what baptism 'does' to the little baby being baptised, let us examine rather what the neophyte, by a presence paradoxical but challenging, can do in and for the receiving Church. And indeed without realising it there is a role to be played. That of being a sign. The newly-baptised witnesses to an act of God not bound by the degree of human consciousness or human capacity that person possesses and which attests God's universal love. But the initial question remains is: how is the baby marked personally, within its being, by what happens to it?

There is only one way to answer this. It is to think of God's action as *progressive*. For the baptism of a newborn child to have sense it must be that the divine action is not completed all at once. And that this is no deviation.

Now this is just what is shown by initiation considered as a whole. It is composed of stages because the gift of God takes our pace. When God acts he never goes straight to the bounds of the possible. That would be inhuman. It would not be divine. God therefore gives us time to welcome his gifts.

What God does in a little child when it is baptised is consequently limited by the human condition of the child at that point. Humanly speaking that child is not nothing. It is still a human being starting out, it forms part of humanity. It is living, included in human solidarity, one of the family. It has symbolic value by its weakness and being wide open to the future. It has taken its place in a world where humanity is trying to arrive and where the Church is present as a sign of the Kingdom. Therefore the child carries weight as a human being.

The divine action stamps the child at the point it has reached. What is baptised in the child is its being such as it is at the present. With the understanding that the child's initiation is not complete and will continue in proportion to the child's human development.

Faith initiated

Adults or newborn children, or again children of school age and young people, all as candidates for initiation, find themselves therefore in a situation where their activity awakens in response to God's action.

Such is under one of its aspects the significance of the christian faith. A person is initiated into the faith by passing through this kind of experience. That allows christians to believe in God not only by giving adherence to his existence and his action but equally by discovering that his intervention in our lives is grace. The initiates give thanks to God for the grace of initiation given them and which gives form to their faith.

On this foundation can be set out the other dimensions of the christian faith. Those initiated are brought to realise that God's gift makes them attentive to the Word, enlightens them on its content and bearing, helps them to break with sin, leads them to opt for Jesus Christ, puts them in solidarity with the christians already initiated, makes them live both in spiritual freedom and in the institutionalised form taken by the Church, brings them finally to the eucharistic act which is thanksgiving and self-oblation. But always it is their re-created free-will which adjusts in this fashion.

The effects of initiation

I have just distinguished the three parties to christian initiation. To end I should like to recapitulate the effects of that initiation as we have observed them on the way.

I shall take care not to reduce these effects to a few general and rather abstract indications. It appears to me indeed that we have allowed what initiation to the faith brings, to become excessively schematised. Often the question raised about baptism in particular,

independently of the rest of the progression. And what we get from
this comes to three factors: salvation, forgiveness of sins, adherence
to the Church. Add to this, that confirmation reinforces this christian
identity and the eucharist feeds it. And there we have how people are
made christian and how they become one.

I do not say that this outline has not the merit of clarity. But I
think it leaves aside some realities which would gain today from being
made more explicit.

Here therefore is how I suggest deploying a little more the effects
of christian initiation.

Dedicated to the Kingdom

I should like to give priority to eschatology, that is the gospel affirmation of the presence of the Kingdom among us, or at least on the
horizon. For it is by this proclamation that the Gosel began historically.
And it is still in this that it finds its strength.

You who have been initiated into the faith of the Gospel, you have
thereby been oriented to the Kingdom to come. You have been dedicated to it. By calling yourselves christians you announce the future God
promises to the world and you affirm that you can and you will be
witnesses to hope in a humanity often apathetic or discouraged.

You have been plunged into baptismal hope in God and you take
the bread and wine of the eucharist, proclaiming the death of Christ
until he comes.

Freed from what has no future

It is eschatology which brings forgiveness. It is the goodness of God
who, seeing the urgency, calls us to live in these last days in the freedom
of children of God who are not expected to carry their burden, and
struggle indefinitely with their past. Christian hope draws life from the
Kingdom of God by experiencing the presence of gospel forgiveness.

This forgiveness does not work by magic, or ingenuously. It allows us
to understand not so much our sin, always complex anyway, as the love
with which God surrounds the world. This love does not wipe out sin
by some feat of messianic power, but puts it behind us, as of little
importance. Like the stones thrown up along the side of the road. Or
like footprints left behind steps going on into tomorrow. If we are forgiven at initiation it is because we are redirected towards the future,
and henceforth our sin dates and has no reason to exist.

A bold undertaking such as this is easily spoilt because we find it
hard to enter into this about-turn. It means for us that we have to hold
fast to our renunciation. If not, our adherence will lack realism. The
Church's prayer for those being initiated expresses the difficulty all

christians find in corresponding to the newness with which God has clothed them.

Able to make remembrance of Christ

To receive the Kingdom of God and break with that counterfeit future which is sin, that requires time. Not time to merit the gift of God. But the indispensable space of time to assimilate stage by stage the gospel mystery.

Christian initiation, consequently, teaches us about time. It makes us enter into the enterprise God has been pursuing for centuries in humanity, and it makes our life enter gradually into the tradition which makes christians. All along the course of initiation we thus go from what is already there and which gives us its stamp, to what we are taking on and which we shall become.

In this way we gradually become creatures of remembrance. We can make real the presence of Jesus in the world. And we can realise in our own individual existence what has been given us, and which we shall never sufficiently apprehend.

As you saw, I propose in this book to consider the ability to make remembrance as being one of the main effects of christian initiation, and one of the actions expressive of the Gospel in us.

God gives himself

Now, turned towards God's future and turned away from our dead-ends of the past, we are initiated into God's generosity. We have not the means to follow this rule of life or to carry out a programme like this on our own. Which is as much as to say that initiation makes us discover what we call the grace of God.

It is a call, a vocation: the catechumens summoned to the sacraments of faith hear it said to them, the children baptised shortly after birth have a way of learning it when the time comes. The grace of God is also the possibility of living by receiving the Word of the Gospel and by giving to our daily actions the sense of a response to the divine initiative. All in all, it is a re-creation of our being. We have been sent back into the world as though everything was beginning again and as though free gift was now the source of our existence. God who has come to dwell with humankind and who calls all to radical renewal, expects of christians that they should be like qualified witnesses of this offer made to all.

Signed in Christ and in his Spirit

To be initiated into the christian faith is therefore to give witness that the presence of God in the world has taken the form of the Gospel

and the Incarnation. And it is to have discovered that we bear in ourselves the Christ of God, so as to constitute with others his present
body.

You have been initiated into the gospel mystery, you are therefore
marked with the sign of Christ and bear within you the form of his life.
His paschal mystery has become yours. From now on his resurrection
has snatched your mortal life from its mortal destiny and anticipates
in it an undreamed-of future. You have received the anointing which
christens.

And in consequence you are henceforth and definitely animated by
the Spirit of Christ who is the Spirit of the Last Days. To speak of that
presence of the Spirit is fundamentally a way of recognising the depths
of your bond with Christ.

An initiating Church

Initiation has at the outset of its programme the discovery of the
Church. At least, a first discovery.

It is not in order to show that the mystery of the Church might be
more simple or more accessible than God's mystery. But it is rather
because it is in the Church that can be found the means of deepening
hope in the Kingdom, receiving forgiveness, and accepting the most profound revelation of Christ and his Spirit.

The initiating Church therefore finds that she is at once a reality *into*
which and *by* which a person is initiated. She points to the mystery of
God but at the same time flows from it. Thus she is in a position to
guide new believers on their journey. She achieves this to the extent
she recognises that she herself is an initiate, in admiration at herself
because full of thanksgiving for her Lord.

Equal and different

The Church of initiation presents herself as a Church for everyone,
with no excepting of persons, no consideration of merits. This is a
Church of the forgiven, and the sense of forgiveness governs the significance which is hers.

A person who is a christian is therefore in principle initiated into the
fundamental equality of believers gathered into a Church. And this
equality is the sign refashioned from the common created state which
all human beings share.

But if we are called to equality because of Jesus Christ the Lord and
Saviour of the world, still we shall not find in the Church a dull, boring,
uniformity. For the christian community is a reception area, an initiation centre. Those who claim to belong to her are therefore not all in

the same position. Among the people who have been received into the Church there are the baptised, but also the catechumens. And among the baptised, some have completed their initiation, others are at the beginning.

It is a pity this is forgotten today. Certainly the baptised are thought of as christians. But those among them who have not been initiated further than baptism are dependent on a pastoral ministry of their own which will respect their situation and not assimilate them to the christians who are initiated. This we can easily accept for children. But it is hardly perceived in regard to adults. The present catechumenal pastorate, as it has developed in France particularly, tries to insist on this. It evinces a kind of affirmation which is far, however, from being the general opinion: it is not baptism which initiates on its own, and initiation represents a specific act which other ecclesial acts cannot replace. When will the Church present herself with the means of genuinely initiating adults who juridically are no doubt no longer catechumens but who are still not 'complete' christians, and who practically speaking are — often — *like* catechumens?

Plunged in the universal

Initiation into the christian faith shows the Church as equally a local reality and at the same time universal. A person is always initiated in this place or in that, brought to the sacraments in a particular ecclesial community. But at the same time, starting from baptism, then in the celebration of confirmation and communion, it is this universality which characterises the christian vocation.

I will content myself with picking out this feature in so far as it is of importance for initiation itself. A person is made a christian in the faith of the whole Church and becomes one by entering into an ecclesial experience opening onto a wider horizon than that of the local community. To be christian is to be plunged into an international Church.

From this point of view it appears to me it would often be useful to recall in one way or another during the initiation process the differences of practice and interpretation between the Churches. In the West the division between Catholics and Reformed christians are not negligible. Whether concerning infant baptism, liturgical rites and signs, or the sacramentality of confirmation. But they are even clearer between western and eastern christianity. As much on the liturgical level as in the understanding of confirmation.

And if making this study appears little suited to the usual possibilities available to initiation, perhaps it would be desirable to do it when making remembrance of baptism and the sacraments of faith received.

The taste and the means
for approaching the sacraments

It is, again, in the Church that we learn in the course of initiation the meaning of the rites and their connection with the faith. To be initiated is to have discovered the liturgy and its place in christian life.

This insight we know does not come immediately to many people. It appears to me it could effectively be linked with the remembrance being formed in the initiated. For this remembrance which is an act of faith and expresses the conviction of belonging to a tradition is expressed through rituals. It becomes a rite so as to be enabled to have practical existence and to be in a position to contribute to hope in the Kingdom.

In this ritual entity extending the whole length of initiation, the three sacraments of initiation stand out. Here again it is plain that initiation ought to bring out the reality of sacramental action. I have partly defined it, on a line with initiation itself, as being that which introduces something new into the continuous series of the rites. Looked at in this way, the sacraments of initiation are what structure the believing memory. They make the christian, because they give the possibilities of becoming a being who remembers and therefore hopes.

Repetition and deepening

Initiation develops as a progression with successive stages. But as I have pointed out, it is not a linear progression properly speaking. It proceeds by revision, repetition, deepening, more than by a succession of new things.

Hence it is anomalous to seek to attribute specific effects to a particular rite, moment, or even sacrament. For at each stage it is the whole of christian values which is in action.

This can be seen in regard to eschatological expectation: an attitude of hope which doubtless takes on characteristic form at baptism but which is equally signified by confirmation and communion. It is the same concerning the ecclesial dimension of faith experience. Or again in what concerns the presence of the Holy Spirit. Or regarding sin: it is 'dealt with' by baptism but it is referred to again within the framework of confirmation and the eucharist.

Consequently, it seems to me that initiation as a whole with its sacraments should have the balance restored, as has been undertaken in our time for the intervention of the Holy Spirit. It has been said repeatedly in the last few years that the Spirit is not only given at confirmation but already in baptism and later in the eucharist. The same can be asserted of the various aspects of christian faith during initiation.

Initiation has a beginning and an end

So now we see what initiation is. It is a progression in the course of which God engenders in us the faith, with its practical possibilities in the Church and in the world.

This progression has a definite beginning. We cannot speak of initiation for the sole reason that someone has begun to draw near to the Gospel. For there to be initiation a request must be made and a Church group must take it up.

Likewise initiation has an end. It is not unending. A point comes when objectively speaking a line must be drawn and the course closed. All is not over, certainly. Christian life will have its share of discoveries and fresh starts. But that will no longer be initiation.

Consequently initiation is an objective operation. It begins and it is completed *when someone says so,* when those initiated and those initiating agree on it. This supposes that a spiritual effort has come to an end but no one can pretend that it is complete. Only, the basic all-important foundations have been put in.

Initiation and re-initiation

The difficulty today is that initiation often remains incomplete. Some baptised persons have not had the opportunity to attend a fundamental course allowing them to develop their faith. Others have gone through their initiation as children and not much of it is left by the time they are grown up.

It appears to me that this situation not only calls for pastoral suggestions which would allow of making a remembrance of the initiation received but above all for proposals of initiation or re-initiation intended for those who desire it. There is here an important responsibility for the Church not fulfilled by the ordinary pastorate for practising or militant christians.

Initiated and initiating

Again, initiation presents itself as a collaboration between those initiating and those who are to be initiated. The transitions made result from a certain amount of discussion between the two groups.

It appears to me that this too is to be listed among the effects of the process. For it reveals christianity as being both an organisation and a personal adventure. These two aspects can enter into varying relations. Sometimes it is the request or the attitude of the candidate anticipating the suggestion from the group. Alternatively the institution has its part in animating and discerning.

In any case, the divide between initiators and initiated is constructive. It maintains that initiation is not simply a personal advance. It makes clear that the initiated are just that when they become aware that the ecclesial experience can give form to something more personal in their life.

A day comes when this christian life can be confirmed. It is the point when the candidates perceive that christianity is not merely the connection of an organisation or a tradition and their own faith but also and at greater depth the paradoxical connection between the objective and the spirit breath of God.

Initiation forms personal faith

In this sense, christian initiation individuates. It gives to each one to exist before God by being called by their christian name and feeling freed. It allows the initiated to find a coherence between the various aspects of their beliefs and the various features of their christian life. The profession of faith expresses unity of conviction, and the numerous postbaptismal rites convey the variety of gifts of the Spirit in the baptised.

I would add that, again, initiation calls to self-knowledge, by some day or other setting the candidates *in face of death*. That of Christ, and therefore their own. Baptism points this out already, the eucharist emphasises it further still. So then, called to hope in the Kingdom, the baptised arrive at recognising that they pass to this future through their own death, opening onto the paschal resurrection.

Is it necessary to add that this individuation of the candidate, very far from individualism turning in on itself, is the condition of real communion in the Church?

Is it necessary, finally, to point out that the christing performed by initiation presupposes initiators who are spiritual, realistic, and available? The Church of today is not so much lacking in potential initiates as patient, humble and clear-headed initiators.

Conclusion

There has been a lot of ground to cover in a delicate and complex subject.

I do not know what impression you will retain of all these considerations. But to end, I should like to state what are for me the main features and which to me appear to point towards the future.

I feel first of all that it is possible, if we will, to restore in the Church a spirituality more plainly baptismal. It only wants each one of us to make remembrance of our own baptism and little by little western christianity can regain its balance. All the more so as our age calls us back to the sources and to the essential.

Next, it appears to me that christian initiation would gain today by being seen as a whole. For the moments of which it is composed affect each other. Our present form of confirmation results from our understanding of baptism, and we celebrate a eucharist which fails to be initiatory because of the oblivion or unease which in practice weighs on baptism.

I also think it is time not to keep initiation any longer for children only. This is no longer possible. A Church conscious of the urgency cannot accept to leave without initiation the numbers of adults appealing to her. But who will have the time, the inclination, the means and the support to dare carry out adaptations in this area?

Equally, it appears to me that the problems of christian initiation become clearer if we admit that we are 'westerners'. We have in our western heritage possibilities which accord with our memory of the past and with our temperament but which we do not always know how to activate. The current difficulties over confirmation are typical of these matters.

Finally, I should like to say that initiation does not constitute the whole of ecclesial responsibility. Obviously. But is it altogether certain that this is not a central and urgent question, at least as much so as others so called?